The Eric Trap

5 Things You Better Get Right as a Leader

Jim Wideman, Sam Luce, and Kenny Conley

with Kristin Englund, Sherri Epperson, Craig Gyergyo, Deana Hayes, and Matt McDaniels

AN INFUSE PUBLICATION

©2012 JIM WIDEMAN MINISTRIES, INC.
2441 Q OLD FORT PARKWAY #354
MURFREESBORO, TN 37128
WWW.JIMWIDEMAN.COM

BUILDING.STRONG LEADERS

Table of Contents

Introduction

Eric pulled into his driveway and shifted his pale blue Ford Focus™ into park. It was the end of a really long day, a day that he was supposed to have off. Quite honestly, Eric couldn't remember the last time he hadn't worked on a Friday. If he didn't love the work so much, he might have resented having to work so hard. However, the pace he'd been going at for the past few months was starting to challenge his passion for the job.

With a detached look on his face, Eric gazed out the window. In his mind, he was recounting all of the previous events of his week. He searched for words to accurately describe all that had happened. *Unreal? Sobering? Overwhelming?* Seconds later, the emotional toll of the week caught up with Eric as he buried his face in his hands and wept. It was a lot; no, it was too much for him to bear.

He thought, *If I were called to ministry, why does the most logical solution seem to be throwing in the towel? If this used to come so natural to me, why is it so hard now?*

Never in his thirty-six years of life had he felt so much pressure and, at the same time, so inadequate. In his mid twenties, he had been part of a thriving team at a start-up ad agency. He worked full time at the agency and volunteered whenever he could at New Hope Community Church as an elementary-boys' small-group leader. He loved his job, but he dreamed of the day that he could work at the church full time. The moments he spent leading that small group of third-through-fifth-grade boys made his week. He was a natural, and he wanted to be able to devote 100 percent of his efforts to kids' ministry.

So, ten years ago, when Eric got the offer to be New Hope's first full-time children's pastor, he was ecstatic. He made sure to seek sound advice and commit the offer to prayer and fasting first, but it quickly became clear to Eric that he had nothing to doubt. He was created for this job. He even found he could incorporate a lot of the skills he had learned from the ad agency into his new job. Success came quickly and naturally, but simply pastoring kids was a dream come true.

The church grew quickly, and Eric was stretched in areas he was unfamiliar with. Fortunately, he valued hard work. He wasn't afraid to take on new challenges. Best of all, he always did what he had to do to get the job done.

However, things were different today. Very different.

Eric leaned into everything that came naturally to him, yet he still found he was coming up short. When he did what he was absolutely best at, he only encountered frustration. Something stopped working, and he just couldn't figure out what it was.

Volunteers were walking away faster than he could recruit new ones. His pastor didn't value what he valued. In fact, his pastor seemed to take the side of those who were against him. Ministry peers empathized with him, but their advice didn't really comfort. Worst of all, Eric's family was just hanging together by a strand. He was inadvertently hurting his children and his wife by issuing ultimatums, something he never imagined several years before. Everything seemed to be crumbling around him. No matter how much or how hard he worked, he couldn't hold it all in place.

"If I'm doing everything right, why is everything falling apart?" Eric questioned. "Why do I just want to quit?"

Since everything had unraveled in the past week, Eric had spent the entire day by himself getting everything ready for the weekend. While doing the job of ten different people, he couldn't shake the thoughts that bombarded his mind all throughout the day.

Is my time in ministry over? Should I begin looking again at ad agencies that are hiring? Will I find a better situation at another church?

All Eric knew was life could not continue the way it was going. Something had to give.

Eric sat in the driveway for a few more minutes gathering the nerve to go inside. He'd told Rebecca he was going to be home in thirty minutes, which was two hours ago. This wasn't going to be pretty, especially after the big fight they'd just had.

Eric opened the door and wiped his eyes. Under his breath he muttered, "This isn't how I imagined any of this."

Sunday

SUNDAY, FEBRUARY 17ᵀᴴ, 6:45 A.M.

It wasn't much different from any other Sunday morning for Eric. Although he wouldn't quite consider himself a "morning person," Eric enjoyed getting to the church early. Typically he'd pull in while it was still dark, several hours before the 9:00 A.M. service. Usually, Eric was the first one there, and he liked it that way.

Others might call it routine or a chore, but Eric considered it therapeutic to move throughout the building in the stillness of the morning turning on lights and adjusting thermostats. Those were the moments that he used to prepare for the day before him. Sometimes Eric would spend this time praying for the programs, the songs, and every little activity that was planned. Most importantly, he used the time to pray for all the laughing and smiling kids who would barge through the doors later that morning.

Specific names and faces came to mind. Under his breath he whispered, "Lord, I pray for Simon today. He's had such a hard year since his parents divorced, and he's really struggling to make friends with the other second and third grade boys. God, I pray that today would be the day that he connects with his peers."

A big smile flashed across Eric's face as he thought about seven-year-old Katie Martin. "Jesus, thank You so much for little Katie's great faith! Thank You for helping her see You and have the courage to ask You into her life last week. Lord, I pray that she not lose the joy of following You."

Eric continued walking the halls completing his mindless tasks amid the blaring silence. His mind wandered from thought to thought, wondering how each preschool lesson would go, if the first and second grade girls were going to like the activity in their small group, and whether Billy was going to pick a fight with Gregory again this week.

His mind also drifted to thoughts far more carnal. He relived the plot twists and cliffhanger endings of the movies he stayed up too late watching. Subconsciously, Eric's mind returned to his personal, never-ending debate of his favorite superhero: Batman or Superman? The heater kicked on loudly and jolted his mind back to the present. His eyes darted around, and he breathed a sign of relief finding safety in the empty hallways. Smiling, he wondered what his kids would think if they really knew what went on in the mind of a children's pastor.

If someone asked Eric which day of the week was his favorite, he'd readily answer Sunday. It was the day he looked forward to most. His staff and volunteers could all readily recite his favorite phrase, "Sunday is a day of promise and potential, a day boys and girls come to experience Jesus." Pretty much everything Eric did all week pointed to Sunday morning. It was the pinnacle of his week.

However, in the safety of those empty corridors, Eric's mind sorted through repressed compartments and pulled out feelings of insecurity and dread. Yes, Sunday was the pinnacle of his week, and it was the day that he got to do the jobs he loved most and was best at. But Sunday was also the day the worst parts of his job also surfaced. No matter how much he wanted those dreaded pests to simply disappear, they were his reality. More than once in the privacy of his home, Eric found himself confessing to his wife, Rebecca, "If I didn't have to deal with the hassle of undependable volunteers or clueless parents, this job would be absolutely perfect."

When Eric was just a volunteer, all he knew was showing up and leading his small group of third-through-fifth-grade boys. He'd prepare for his lesson for days, and the forty minutes he had with them was the highlight of his week. When Eric came on staff, he naively thought that that forty minutes of pure joy would translate to forty hours of the same. He didn't expect the constantly complaining parents asking him why the church didn't do this or why the church did do that. Eric got a fair share of compliments and praises, but he couldn't figure out why those select few parents could sap his joy so quickly. A run-in with two or three of those parents quickly sent him to a dark place.

Even worse were the volunteers. Most of them showed up on New-Hope time (i.e., five minutes before church began—well after most of the kids were already there). It didn't matter how many times he begged and pleaded with them to arrive twenty minutes early, they always showed up when they felt like it, if they showed up at all. On Saturdays, Eric cringed every time his phone rang. On average, three to four volunteers would call to let him know that they would not be there the next day. Some had legitimate excuses; some didn't. Some volunteers didn't even call. Whether they actually forgot they were on the schedule or just ignored their duties because of a better opportunity, Eric never knew. Usually he didn't ask either. Somehow it felt better to assume an emergency or sickness rather than face the reality that something they'd rather do came up.

Truth be told, Eric was a bit of a pushover. Sure, his pastor would be hard pressed to find a guy as kind and caring as Eric Newman. And he would be unlikely to find anyone with something bad to say about Eric, well, beside those few parents with their weekly list of complaints. But Eric didn't rock the boat. When a herd of late volunteers ran into the classrooms at the last minute, Eric would let out a sigh of relief and say, "I can't tell you how glad I am to see you!" Only later would he send his volunteers a blanket e-mail not singling anyone out but reminding all of them to be early each week.

In the darkness and stillness of that early Sunday morning, inevitably Eric's thoughts exposed what he dreaded most: *Which volunteers are not going to show up today? We're a little low on help this morning, but if everyone shows up, we can just about cover every room. Wait, who am I kidding? Everyone never shows up on the same week, and I'm going to spend the first fifteen minutes of both services shuffling volunteers around, and at least one of our rooms is going to have a whacked-out ratio of children to teachers. I'll walk on the stage of Kids Church five minutes late and drenched in sweat, just like every Sunday.*

As Eric finished up his duties around the church, he reflected on the stillness of that Sunday morning. He loved that early Sunday-morning solitude and the extra time to think, pray, and contemplate. He considered it his time to just be. However, more often than not, it ended up being the calm before the storm—that raging storm that came every seventh day at 9:00 A.M. and 11:00 A.M.

Sunday truly was the best day of his week, but buried in the background was a constant sense of dread. It was an ever-present dread that made Sundays so much less than what they were supposed to be for Eric Newman.

9:04 A.M. THE MELTDOWN

So far, so good. Although service technically began almost five minutes ago, there was a steady stream of kids still checking in to their classrooms. Surprisingly, almost all the volunteers Eric expected to show up actually made it, requiring only minor shuffling; however, Eric's real problem was just entering the building.

JIM SWANSON

Jim was probably the most talented volunteer Eric had ever known. He had been serving in kidmin much longer than Eric; although, he'd only been at New Hope Community Church for three years. Jim was downright gifted when it came to children's ministry. He was a skilled communicator to large groups of kids. He was funny; he was able to break down complicated concepts into a language that kids could understand. When he spoke, kids hung on to every word. For this reason, he was the primary teacher or emcee in kids' church at the 9:00 A.M. service. Usually he and Eric would take turns teaching the kids: when Jim was teaching, Eric would emcee; and when Eric was teaching, Jim would emcee. When Eric was sick or out of town, he could usually count on Jim to cover all the services. It was a great deal, except that Jim was becoming more and more undependable.

Here it was already five minutes past nine, and Jim was just walking in. Granted, all the kids were in small groups at this time, and Jim didn't go on stage for another ten minutes, but with Jim walking in so late, he and Eric would not get any time to talk about their transitions, much less rehearse. If this only happened occasionally, Eric would have probably been a little more understanding, but this was becoming a weekly occurrence.

Eric was furious. He'd been watching the clock since 8:50. While helping kids check in and glancing in on various classrooms, Eric had been peeking out the window to see if Jim had arrived. He had even walked through the lobby three or four times in the past fifteen minutes to make sure Jim wasn't making small talk with one of the greeters. Eric never worried that Jim would not show up, but he always fretted over his arrival time. Sometimes there were changes or adjustments that needed to be made to the service, but Jim's late arrival made discussions about these changes nearly impossible.

It would probably be different if this were just a personality quirk. Every ministry had those right-brained, creative-type volunteers that couldn't arrive on time even if their lives depended on it. Although he and Jim had never specifically talked about it, Eric didn't get the impression with Jim that this was a personality quirk. There seemed to be some unspoken tension between them. Conversations were never deeper than casual dialogue or short talks about ministry tasks. Jim was never early, and he usually left in a hurry to meet his family for the 11:00 A.M.

service. He rarely showed up to special trainings or volunteer social events. He never returned phone calls or e-mails; although, he inadvertently acknowledged receiving them by always being prepared on Sunday.

It was this awkward and unspoken tension that bothered Eric. There was obviously something going on, but Jim wasn't being honest. What really bugged Eric was that Jim seemed to be wasted potential. Jim was absolutely amazing with the kids. Depending on budget growth, Eric was considering bringing someone on staff in the next year, and it would be ideal if it were someone who could direct and lead the elementary program, something that Jim would be perfect for.

Not hiring Jim would create even more awkwardness because it would be obvious to everyone that Jim would be the perfect fit for the new position. Although no one other than the staff knew that this was a possible scenario, Eric realized that this might become a very sticky situation. If Eric hired someone else, Jim would probably be offended. Perhaps he'd even leave the church. Parents and volunteers would certainly question why Jim wasn't considered. Eric's only thoughts were to look at hiring for another position so that he could avoid the relational fallout. The problem with that was that he really needed an elementary director more than any other role. Eric constantly questioned, "Why did this have to be so complicated? Why couldn't Jim just be more cooperative?"

But today was different. Today, Eric had some information that he didn't have last week. Jim had been talking, and it wasn't pretty.

The week before Eric and his wife of fourteen years, Rebecca, had joined Kurt and Jeanne Martin for dinner. Rebecca and Jeanne have been close friends for many years. Every couple of months the two families get together, but the girls typically do lunch or coffee on a weekly basis. In addition to her friendship with Rebecca, Jeanne has been a first- and second-grade girls' small-group leader for the last two years. Eric had recruited her one night as their families got together for dinner. Jeanne was one of his best volunteers—always on time, prepared, and enthusiastic about serving. At these family get-togethers, both Kurt and Rebecca often felt left out because the conversation always seemed to revolve around specific children, curriculum issues, or ideas for improvements.

At this last dinner though, Jeanne had shared some concerning news with Eric. "This isn't meant to be gossip or anything like that, but I really think you should have a conversation with Jim Swanson. The sooner the better."

"Why, what's wrong with Jim?" Eric had asked as if he knew of nothing that was wrong. Had others noticed the tension they shared? Had Jeanne?

Jeanne leaned in and then had said, "I've never thought too much about it, but I've noticed that something seems to be off with him." She paused, then continued, "Don't get me wrong; he's absolutely amazing with the kids, and he does such a great job teaching the lesson and setting up us small-group leaders for success. As good as he is, it just doesn't seem that his heart is in it like I've seen before. Although I'm pretty occupied with my girls once they start arriving, I notice that he seems to be in and out for his part and that is it. The girls loved it when he used to pop into our group to cut up for a few minutes or further explain a point he spoke about when he taught. I know that other groups really liked that as well, but he doesn't seem to be around for that anymore. I know that this probably wasn't something he was supposed to do, but it was a nice touch, and we miss it."

None of this had been new information to Eric. He'd never told Jim to visit the small groups; it was just something Jim thought of doing a long time ago. It was his thing, and it further endeared the kids to him. Eric had noticed that Jim was doing this less and less; and in recent months, he hadn't been doing it at all. Eric had a hard time believing that was the reason Jeanne thought he should talk to Eric.

And then Jeanne had taken a more serious tone and continued, "So on Monday I ran into Jim at the grocery store. It was a treat to be able to talk to him for a few minutes since I rarely get to talk to him on Sundays anymore, but he said something that really alarmed me. I told him how much I enjoyed his teaching the week before on the prodigal son, especially the story he'd told about his own past wandering from faith. He seemed appreciative, but he quickly dismissed my compliment saying how frustrated he was with the new curriculum and how much he wished we were using what we used last year or would at least look into something else. It sounded like he's put a lot of thought into it, and he had some ideas of other options."

"I'm well aware of Jim's dislike of the new curriculum. He tells me every week," Eric had quickly replied. "What Jim doesn't see is how much better the experience is for you and all the other small-group leaders. Jim and I are strong teachers; we can work with and modify the teaching scripts. My focus is on making sure the small-group leaders have what they need."

"No, I get that," Jeanne had continued. "I even told him that. I told him that most of us small group leaders are loving it."

"He'd probably know that if he were still visiting all the small groups like he used to," Eric had slung back. Eric had regretted saying that out loud as soon as the words left his mouth. A quick look at Rebecca's disapproving stare meant she had felt the same way.

Jeanne had gone on, seeming not to notice Eric's dig at Jim. "I told him that I thought his teaching was as good as it was last year with the old curriculum. He thanked me and said that it just took a lot more work. However, he said that you and he disagreed on the curriculum choice, and in reality, that his opinion didn't matter because you were the children's ministry czar, and we were only going to do what you wanted to do, no matter how 'out of touch' you were with what was really going on. Eric, I was really troubled by what he said about you. He didn't say any of this maliciously. They were almost dismissive statements. Why would he call you a czar, and why would he say this to me? I just thought I'd tell you as soon as I could. Whatever is going on, I'm sure you'd want to deal with it."

Eric had calmly dismissed Jeanne with, "Wow, I'm not sure where that's coming from. Maybe Jim's got some stuff he's going through and what he said is a reaction to that. I'll get with him soon and see if we can't talk through our differences." Underneath the surface, though, Eric had been boiling. He had done his best to subdue his emotions while at the Martin's, but once in the car, he had totally unleashed his anger and frustrations to Rebecca.

Now that the awkwardness was out in the open, he was going to have to deal with it. What bothered Eric most was that he didn't know if Jim had talked to anyone else. Was it just Jeanne, or were there others? Jeanne was very loyal to Eric, but would others support Eric the way that Jeanne had? The fact that Jeanne's account was the first he'd heard told him that either Jim hadn't talked to anyone else, or he had talked, but those people weren't talking to Eric. Did they agree with Jim?

At that point, Eric had resolved to himself, "As far as I'm concerned, Jim is done. I've got to deal with his poison before there's an all-out coup."

"Hey, Jim, running a little late, aren't we?" Eric remarked as he approached Jim.

With a wry smile, Jim bounced back, "You know how it is."

"No, Jim, I'm not sure I do. You know I've asked you to be here by 8:40, but you've not been here that early since September when we kicked off the new curriculum."

Jim stared expressionless at Eric.

"Listen, can you hang around after the lesson today?" Eric said quickly filling the awkward silence. "Lately you've been taking off right after we break into small groups, and I don't see you again until the next week. I have something that I'd really like to talk to you about."

Jim interrupted, "Eric, I've told you this before; I have to run home and pick up my family to get them here in time for the 11:00 service."

"I remember. I just don't understand what changed. You used to stay for the whole service, but now you don't. You guys have two cars, don't you? You don't have to pick up your family every Sunday. I feel like you're barely here. I've got important stuff to talk to you about, but you're twenty-five minutes late, and now you're leaving thirty minutes before the service lets out. When are we supposed to talk?"

Eric regretted beginning this conversation in the hallway as soon as Jim started to raise his voice, "Hey, chill out, Eric. Service just started a few minutes ago, and I'm still fifteen minutes early for my part."

"No, we're supposed to be on stage in ten minutes, and I've been asking you for months to be here at 8:40. You're twenty-five minutes late."

Jim rolled his eyes. "Fine, I'm twenty-five minutes late. I'm sorry I'm not here at the time you demand. I'll try better next time."

"No you're not, and what do you mean by 'the time I demand'?"

Jim crossed his arms, "Eric, what's this all about anyway? Where are you going with all of this?"

Eric glanced around, seriously regretting this conversation as parents and volunteers snuck glances at the heated conversation building in the hallway. "I told you Jim, I'd rather talk to you after the service, maybe during small-group time. NOW is not the time, and THIS certainly isn't the place."

"Hey, I didn't start this conversation; you did. Besides, I already told you, I have to go pick up my family otherwise they'll be late for service."

"What about later after the 11:00 service? Would that work?"

"No, Eric, that's not going to work. I've got lunch plans."

"You don't have any flexibility at all? Jim, isn't there something you can work out?"

"Are you serious?"

"Jim, I feel that if we don't talk today, I won't see you again until next week. I want to talk with you today."

"Well, Eric, it's not always about you and what you want."

"What's that supposed to mean?"

Jim raised his voice even more, "Exactly what you think it means. You're a control freak, Eric. Ask anyone around here," he said while motioning to parents and volunteers passing in the hallway. "You call all the shots without any input from anyone. Even when we have suggestions, they fall on deaf ears unless it's something you already want to do."

"That's not true!" Eric shot back.

"Yes, it is. It's been true for me, and I've seen you do it with others."

Eric pointed his finger at Jim, "Don't make this all about the curriculum we switched to this year. I know you don't like it, but you've got to think about the small-group leaders too. You're not the only one in that room every Sunday."

"This isn't just about the curriculum; you've got your controlling fingers on everything; and this has been going on for as long as I've been here. However, you've been a real pill about this curriculum. Ever since you came back from that conference, you decided that it was the way you were going to go; no questions asked. Yeah, I don't like it, and yes, it is a better option for the small-group leaders. I just wanted to know if we could explore other options, maybe find something that works better for both, but you don't care. Your mind was already made up."

Eric stood motionless, fuming with frustration and anger. Words escaped him.

Jim pointed his finger back at Eric, lightly jabbing it into his chest. "Eric, you may think you're running a good show here, but it's not working. It might all look good on the outside, but it's a glorified one-man show. When I signed up, I thought I was joining New Hope Community Church's children's ministry, not the Eric Newman Show. I'm not going to be your puppet!"

Sweat began to bead up on Eric's red forehead. "I never asked you to be my puppet. I don't ask that of anyone. I'm the leader here, and, ultimately, I have to call some shots and make some decisions because I'm responsible, not you."

"That's where you're wrong, Eric. Your thinking is all messed up."

"I'm messed up?" Eric pointed at himself and took a step back. "I'm not the one calling people names and spreading poison about other people."

"What are you talking about?"

"Jeanne told me about your conversation at the supermarket. She told me how you think I'm 'out of touch.' Oh, and you're calling me a czar? Really? Are we in middle school again? Have we resorted to name calling?"

Silence.

Jim stared into Eric's face with a grim look of indifference.

Jim broke the silence. "You know what, Eric? I'll make this easy for you." In a quick movement, Jim removed his lanyard and tossed it against Eric's chest. The well-worn and weathered lanyard fell to the floor. "I'm done. Have fun with your show." Jim turned and began walking away.

"Really, you're walking away?" Eric called out.

Jim turned back, "Eric, face the truth. This should have happened a long time ago."

With that, Jim made an about-face and marched out the church doors, jumped in his car, and left New Hope.

Time seemed to stand still. The vivid confrontation had silenced the hallway. Eric felt dozens of eyes boring into him.

Did that really just happen?

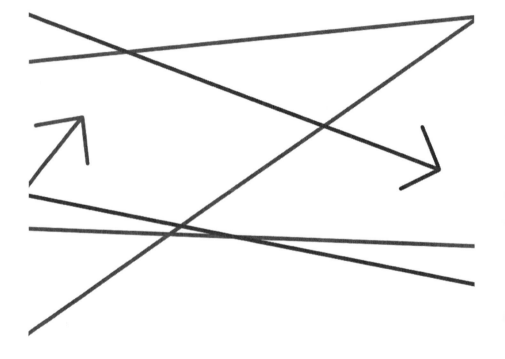

Chapter 1: Delegation

CRAIG GYERGYO

Several years ago, I had the opportunity to be a summer intern at a church in my hometown. I was really excited about this particular opportunity because the senior pastor of this church happened to be one of my personal church heroes. All summer long, I followed in the footsteps of this wonderful leader as we ministered to kids at camps, went on mission trips, and delved into all of the business of the church. That summer I spent hours upon hours with this hero of mine. We shared a cabin at camp and a cot in a rundown hotel room in Mexico. (It doesn't get much closer than that, folks.) I walked away from that internship a better minister and leader than I was when I began. It was truly a thrill to serve alongside this man that I had looked up to for so many years. I learned how to communicate the gospel more effectively, and I observed as this pastor masterfully planned and executed faith-rich programs for kids of all ages. I was in awe (and still am).

Ninety-five percent of what I learned about ministry that summer was from the pastor's example. I learned lessons on everything from the importance of keeping a timely schedule to leading worship. As for the other five percent of my "summer education," well, no one is perfect, right? Early on, it was clear that this pastor liked to do things himself—with no help from anyone else, thank you. For instance, one day while in the office, the pastor gave me a to-do list. The list included, among other things, database work. The pastor took time to explain to me exactly what he wanted me to do. He began to tell me exactly which information was important to enter into the database and how to do the job. Then, abruptly, the pastor stopped what he was saying, looked at me, and said, "You know what? This job is going to take you twelve hours to complete, but it will only take me about an hour and a half . . . outta my way." Just like that, my to-do list got a little bit shorter. This was the beginning of a trend. Throughout the summer, items from my task list were transferred from my file to his.

You're probably thinking, well, maybe you were just not up to the task. (It wouldn't be the first time that someone accused me of that, by the way. Did I mention that I work at a church?) In the right circumstances, this accusation could be true of any of us, but in this case we are talking about tasks such as data entry and organizing camp skits. It's not as if he were asking me to fly a group of fifth-grade boys from the campfire to the moon in a rocket ship. No, this pastor had an underlying belief that he would often quote: "If you want something done right, you've got to do it yourself."

How many of us subscribe to that same thinking? Far too many of us if the truth be told. Contrary to what we tell volunteers, parents, and staff; we all too often believe deep down that we are the best (and maybe the only) people to do the job right. Sure, we'll allow someone else to sort the popsicle sticks into bins or maybe let someone else decide which toppings to get on the pizza now and again, but all of the really big stuff—the important stuff—is left for us. That means that the lesson making, speaking, teaching, e-mailing, recruiting, advertising, praying, and all other verbs associated with our ministry that have the -ing suffix are our jobs. Why? Because if you want something done right, you've got to do it yourself. That's why.

There's something that you and I need to know. Make sure that you are sitting down for this because you may find this to be surprising: GOD NEVER INTENDED FOR ONE PERSON TO RUN THE ENTIRE CHILDREN'S MINISTRY. Though Jesus, in fact, did say, "Let the little children come to Me" (Matt. 19:14), I don't believe that it was his intention to be a solo act. You see, the Scriptures compare the church to a body. A body has many different parts, and those many different parts have many different functions. All come together under one head, however, to work in a concerted fashion. A heart cannot do what a stomach can do; a mouth cannot do what an ear can do, and so forth. Still, all of these body parts are indispensable to the functioning of a healthy body. So it should be with the church.

The healthy church or ministry looks like a body with many different people bringing many different gifts and talents together under one head—the Lord Jesus—to work in unison and bring God's kingdom here on earth as it is in heaven. What would our churches look like if we took steps toward forming a community of people with God-given gifts and talents within our ministries rather than staging a one-person show? Our ministries would look a lot more like what God intended. In order to make this vision a reality, we have to be willing to delegate and start acting on our belief that God has created the church and all ministry with a team in mind.

Delegation is as old as human history. It's right there in Genesis 2. God creates the heavens and the earth, the sun, the moon, and the stars, as well as, hordes of living creatures. After kicking back to rest a spell, the Author of the universe who has just created everything out of nothing, turns to His prized creation, Adam, and says, "I've got a job for you" (or something along those lines). Given Adam's limited resume coupled with the brand-newness of, well, everything, we'd imagine that the Lord is about to ask Adam to dust the fig trees, feed the Venus flytraps, or do some other menial task. Instead, God gives Adam a job that is going to (A) take lots of creativity and (B) have ramifications for all of eternity. Right there in Genesis 2:19-20, God gives Adam the task of naming the animals—all of them. The Scriptures tell us that God brought the birds, reptiles, mammals, amphibians, and all other critters to Adam, and He had Adam give out names to each creature.

Have you ever wondered why God, the Lord of earth and heaven, the Creator of all things, would give the job of naming the animals to a guy who had literally no experience? I mean, Adam hadn't even learned to brush his teeth and comb his hair at this point, and here he is making up names that are going to stick for all time. Some of you are thinking, How hard could it be? Just a few names, right?

How many of you are like me and had to consult eighteen different books along with casting lots just to come up with a name for your third child? Considering that Adam didn't have the benefit of an animal-names book to confer with, one might begin to wonder, why Adam? God may as well have just let the animals name themselves. But not our God. He gave still-wet-behind-the-ears Adam that huge responsibility.

Why would God do such a thing? I believe that God had a much bigger picture in mind than just a bunch of names. Sure, allowing Adam to name the animals would mean that names like aardvark and platypus will be around for all time, but perhaps God wasn't as concerned with the outcome as He was the process. You see, God trustfully delegated an important job to Adam because He wanted to see Adam grow more fully into the person He had created him to be. God knew that this particular work was going to draw something out of Adam that merely dusting the fig trees could never do. God used delegation as a people-development mechanism. Through the task of naming animals, Adam develops his creativity and decision-making skills. He grew in his ability to manage a mammoth (pun intended) task and, no doubt, practiced the skills of editing and revising. The spelling of hippopotamus was destined to stump grade-school kids for generations, but that wasn't the main issue. Adam growing into the person who God created him to be was the main issue.

God didn't just delegate a task either. He delegated authority along with the task. The Bible says that "whatever the man called each living creature, that was its name" (Gen. 2:19). No looking over Adam's shoulder by God. No second-guessing his decisions. No final sign off necessary. God passed the authority squarely on to Adam. God was the One who imagined each creature. He decided how many legs each would have, what color their skin or fur would be, and if they could swim, fly, or trot. It was He who fluffed feathers, painted beaks, and orchestrated each grunt, growl, and hoot. God would be the best and logical choice to name the animals as He knew each creature intimately. But despite all of this, He trusted Adam with the job of naming His wonderful creations.

Examples of God's delegation aren't limited to the Garden of Eden either. Elsewhere in the Scriptures we find Jesus after three brief years of earthshaking ministry and disciple making, turning his Father's business over to a bunch of fishermen, tax collectors, and other rather common folks. How many of us would struggle to let someone name our pet rock, let alone our ministry? Or how many of us would be willing to loosen the death grip that we hold on our large-group program so that a volunteer can lead in our place? Yet, if we're following the example that the Lord has set for us from the very beginning of time, we'd be quick to entrust the business of the ministry to others because, after all, that's what He did. That means not just entrusting others with counting out sets of pipe cleaners or making copies, but entrusting others with the big things—jobs such as writing or editing curriculum, communicating lessons to large groups, leading meetings, and recruiting volunteers.

I am not suggesting that we abdicate our calling by delegating every ounce of our role and authority. No, there are matters that require our hands-on leadership. Besides, the point of delegation is not to make it so that we have absolutely no work to do. The point of delegation is to free us to do what only we can do. Moreover, delegated authority should always reflect the vision of the ministry and mirror the values that we hold as overseers of the ministry. What I am suggesting is that we allow others to exercise their God-given gifts and talents whenever we have opportunity, for we are empowering the church to truly be the church when we do so.

One of the most celebrated sports teams in modern history is the United States Olympic men's basketball team of the 1992 summer games, also known as the "Dream Team." The story of the Dream Team begins with a team of U.S. amateurs who had finished in a disappointing third place during the Seoul games of 1988. As inventors of the game, Americans had always enjoyed a place at the very top, internationally speaking, of the basketball heap. However, as the game of basketball spread and developed in other nations, the gap between the U.S. and everyone else had seemingly dwindled away to nothing. Then in 1989, new rules emerged that allowed professional basketball players to participate in the forthcoming Olympics. From there, the U.S. gathered perhaps the greatest talent ever assembled on a basketball court. The team featured Earvin "Magic" Johnson, Larry Bird, and Michael Jordan among others. The rest is sporting history. Led by Coach Chuck Daly, the Dream Team dismantled the competition at a furious pace on their way to earning a gold medal and restoring the pride of an entire nation.

The Dream Team was some collection of talent. Could there be a better trio than Magic, Bird, and Jordan—the playmaking skills of Magic Johnson, plus the inside-outside precision shooting of Larry Bird, not to mention the above-the-rim excitement of Michael Jordan? The best part was these mega-superstars put aside their own egos and agendas to work as a team under Coach Daly's direction and vision. I'd take those guys in a pick-up game for sure! Maybe they could even make a guy with a jump shot as bad as mine look good.

Okay, I admit, I will never be a part of a basketball Dream Team, but you and I can be part of the ministry equivalent. What if you were to design your own ministry Dream Team from scratch? What would it look like? What talents and gifts would you need to have represented in your group? To whom would you ideally delegate responsibility and authority?

Actually, it's not a question of *what if* you could design a ministry Dream Team; it's a matter of *where* to start. As you begin to design your ministry Dream Team, sit down with a group of your core leaders (you wouldn't do this alone, would you?); and begin to brainstorm the roles, jobs, gifts, and talents that need to be represented within your ministry in order for you to be most effective. Likely, you'll need everyone from A/V people to small-group leaders to set builders in your ministry. Make a list of every role that you can think of that needs to be filled.

Next, begin to write role descriptions for each job. You'll want to include the *what, where, when*, and *how* of each job on your role descriptions. Give plenty of details so that anyone can readily know what the expectations for each role are on the front end. Be sure not to go overboard, however, as these role descriptions are for volunteers. Keep your role descriptions as brief and desirable and doable as possible.

Then the fun really begins. Fill the roles with people whose gifts and talents match what you are looking for to begin comprising your Dream Team. To be sure, this is most often neither a fast process nor an easy one. As much as we'd like for the entire team to be in place within a couple of days, the truth is that we are looking at a process that will last a number of months at the very least. The key to the entire process is prayer—prayer that conforms your heart to the Lord's heart; prayer that gives you eyes to see as He sees. The importance of prayer in this instance cannot be overstated. We are humbly dependent on God's leading, God's grace, and God's provision in assembling our Dream Team. It's all too easy to lose sight of the importance of prayer in today's fast-paced church life. If you've fallen away from regular prayer, let this quest to have a Dream Team be something that helps to get you back on track.

Once you have committed to prayer and made your role descriptions, set out to get to know as many people as you can in your church and elsewhere. Introduce yourself to folks at church events, strike up conversations with people who you recognize at the grocery store, search your database for people whose profile matches your needs, and then give them a call. And with the exception of the shower, take your role descriptions along with you everywhere you go. (Remember that bit about being ready "in and out of season"?)

Some will stop short of taking these steps because they don't want to give people the impression that they are "using them." I've heard this line of thinking expressed before, and I'd like to help strip away this fear if it is one of yours. If you truly are just "using" people, then, by all means, please do stop! I am sure that none of us wants to be guilty of using people for selfish reasons. But, if you believe deep down that God wants to do something in the lives of men, women, teens, boys, and girls; then take these steps. Look to get people involved in the life of the church because you believe in delegation as people development. I'm sure that Team USA had a blast finding the right guys for their team, and God wants nothing less for you.

For a long time, I searched for somebody or something to take our large-group program to the next level. Our program was fun, and kids were certainly hearing from God's Word on a week-to-week basis. But, I had this sneaking suspicion that we were only scratching the surface of what we could do. Our dream was to create an experience for kids that was memorable, creative, powerful, and compelling. We had recently added a live worship component to the program, and that, coupled with the teen and adult communicators that we had assembled, gave me the sense that the sky was the limit. I began to pray about how the large-group program could take the next step. Truth be known, I wasn't even sure what I was praying for, but I knew that I trusted God and that He had a plan for the large-group program.

Lo and behold, one day I was reading through new volunteer applications when I came across Kim's information. As I read Kim's application, one thing jumped out to me right away—she was a producer for a local news station. Bingo! I knew just the role for Kim. I met her in person soon after our new-volunteer orientation and told her about our large-group program. I shared the vision for the large-group program with her and asked if she'd be interested in coming to check out what we were doing. She agreed to do just that, and soon after that Kim joined our large-group team. I have been more than happy to delegate the responsibility of editing scripts and directing volunteers in this environment to Kim because she has gifts and experience in this area that I could never replicate. Do I still give input regarding the large-group program? Sure. But I do so bearing in mind that Kim is my large-group producer. With her leadership, the best is yet to come for this program.

Ultimately, delegation happens in the context of relationships. God had a relationship with Adam in the Garden of Eden, and Jesus certainly had a relationship with His disciples. In both cases, the delegation of responsibility comes with authority. Also, in both examples, the delegator holds people development as a main priority. I am doing my best to follow this example as I serve alongside Kim in our large-group program. Yes, the program is important, but equally important is Kim's development as a Christ follower. I suspect that God wants to do something both in her and through her as she engages as a leader in our large-group program. In this case everybody wins: the ministry benefits by having a more effective large-group program, the kids hear God's Word in a more compelling fashion, and Kim grows in her faith in Christ.

Remember how my church hero assigned me a task that supposedly would take me half a day to complete? He actually reluctantly let go of the reins and let me take on that assignment. Get this; I finished it in less time than the pastor said that it would take him to complete it. I guess you don't have to do something yourself to have it done right after all. This is a lesson on delegation that I will certainly never forget—and how could I given that I married my church hero's daughter! My father-in-law is a wise leader and, like all wise leaders, he has learned to delegate.

We delegate because we're mindful of the fact that God designed ministry with a team in mind. We delegate authority along with responsibility because we believe in delegating as a means of people development. Isn't it time that you begin to delegate more? Start designing your ministry Dream Team, and then watch God go to work.

Your Eric Trap

Don't fall into the same trap as Eric. Go beyond reading inspirational words and stories, and measure your life and ministry against the traps many in ministry fall into as did Eric. Open up your journal or notebook, and take time to answer the questions below. Allow the principles in this chapter to translate into the context of your life and ministry.

Make a list of the top-ten tasks you regularly spend time working on. Isolate five items on your list that can be done by others. Start listing people you know who can take on those jobs.

Who do you know that does a great job of involving others in the work of the ministry? Schedule a lunch meeting with that person, and ask them every question that you can think of regarding delegation.

Who is missing from your Dream Team? Write out a role description for that position, and begin praying that God will provide the right person for that role. Begin making contacts with likely candidates.

How much does what you do in your ministry depend on prayer? Is going to God in prayer about ministry needs or situations a regular habit for you? How can this become something that happens on a regular basis?

What's one area of the ministry where you feel the greatest sense of ownership? What steps can you take to empower others to lead alongside of you in this area?

Where are you currently delegating tasks without delegating authority?

Monday

MONDAY, FEBRUARY 18TH, 7:45 A.M.

Eric hit snooze for the third time straight. Had this been any other Monday, he would have kept hitting the snooze until noon. After a day like yesterday, he probably would have taken a personal day.

Not only was his head still spinning from the disaster that was yesterday's weekend service, but Eric had a standing appointment every other Monday with his pastor, and today was that Monday. Eric's head was still pounding with the words Jim threw his way. Eric muttered to himself, "The nerve that man had. How could Jim even think those things, much less say them, and *in public* for that matter?"

Eric stumbled downstairs. He could smell the coffee brewing. Rebecca, although long gone, had set the timer on his coffeemaker. She'd been sweet even though Eric had not. Jim's words had ruined Eric's day, so he came home in a foul mood and ruined everyone else's day. The only relief the Newman family got was that Eric went to bed early.

Eric considered himself a coffee fanatic. Others might call him a coffee snob. He didn't care. His morning cup of joe did wonders to ground him in reality. Rebecca had brewed his favorite, Sumatra. Despite the way he had treated her and the kids the day before, she still made sure he got exactly what he needed. Any other morning, he would have been at peace with the universe. However, this morning was different. It wasn't just yesterday's events; it was something more; and Eric couldn't put his finger on it. It made him anxious, and the Sumatra didn't help.

Jim is misguided and uninformed, Eric thought. *If he could walk in my shoes for*

a week, he'd know what it was like. He'd take back all those things he said. He'd
appreciate me a little more.

Eric took a slow sip of his coffee. *Does anyone else feel the same as Jim does?*

9:04 A.M. THE COMMUTE

Eric lived six miles from the church. Typically he could pull out of the garage and
be sitting in his office chair within twelve minutes. This morning was far from
typical because of one factor: traffic.

While sitting in the parking lot that was Highway 610, Eric decided to take a
peek at his e-mail. He grabbed his phone and opened up the mail application.
This wasn't going to be pretty. He had avoided his e-mail yesterday as he knew
someone would have something to say about his confrontation with Jim. He
braced himself as he opened his inbox.

Dread overcame him. His shoulders sagged, and he let out a slow and quiet moan. He
was deflated. He set his phone down, put both hands on the wheel, pressed his head
back into the headrest, and closed his eyes. *This is just getting stupid*, he thought.

Eric became lost in his thoughts while reliving all his recent decisions. Although
it seemed like only moments later, honking horns brought him back to reality.
Traffic was moving again. Eric caught up with the cars in front of him just in time
to stop again.

He picked up his phone again and reluctantly opened the new e-mail from
Christine Anderson, his preschool director; it was titled "Resignation."

> Pastor Eric,
> I would like to start by thanking you for the opportunity to serve in your kids'
> ministry. This morning was very enlightening for me as someone who works for

the church. I feel it is my responsibility to inform you that I am unable to continue working as the preschool director for kids' church. It is a tough decision because I love the kids, but over the past few months, it has become clear that things are going to be done a certain way, and I don't feel I can be on board with that direction. I have written this letter and deleted it more times than you know, but after what happened this morning with Jim, it made things clearer in my mind and gave me the strength to hit send. I wish you and your ministry the best of luck.

Sincerely,

Christine Anderson

Eric put his phone down and stared forward. He didn't feel anxious or angry or frustrated, just numb. Traffic began moving again, and he finished his drive into the office. He was on autopilot; his mind was somewhere else. He pulled into his parking space and just sat there for a few minutes trying to figure out how all of this could be happening.

"I just don't get it!" he exclaimed out loud. "Why now?"

Overwhelmed by the content of the email message, Eric hadn't noticed that Christine has copied his boss. Things were about to get even more interesting.

Eric opened his door and got out of his car. He walked through the front doors of the church building and headed toward his office just like he did every day. It was past nine, so he knew the office was going to be busy and filled with staff getting an early start processing the weekend and planning the next weekend. Additionally, there would be teams of volunteers who helped out on Monday mornings counting the offering, processing prayer requests, and putting welcome letters together. The last thing Eric needed right now was to walk into a busy office. He wasn't ready for water-cooler conversations about what went down with Jim, especially after the e-mail he had just read from Christine. Eric approached the office suite and cringed when he heard the commotion of a busy Monday morning.

Instinctively, Eric hung an immediate right and jogged around the preschool hallway so he could come in the back entrance by the bathrooms where his office was in the back corner. Eric quietly opened the back door to the suite and made a break for it. His door was ten paces away. Without looking to the left or the right, he speed walked with determination and purpose toward his sanctuary. Without breaking stride, he pulled out his keys and prepared himself for a quick entry.

At that moment he regretted his decision from a month ago to change the lock on his office door. Over the past few months, he'd noticed the candy he kept in his office disappearing. More than likely, the culprits were teenagers. Jake, the student pastor, constantly had teenagers in and out of the offices on Wednesday nights even though he'd been told on multiple occasions to keep the office suite locked. Since Eric had the lock changed, the candy stopped disappearing, but the extra keys on his ring made it difficult to locate the right one immediately. Finally, Eric found the right one and pushed the door open in a sweeping motion. He was in.

"Pastor Eric?"

Busted! Eric stared straight ahead into his office, unable to move. The office looked more like a storage closet. Actually, it looked more like what a storage closet would throw up. Eric kept telling the staff that he was going to reorganize, but a busy summer turned into a busy fall and the "stuff" of ministry remained in his office where it fell.

"Pastor Eric?"

It was Florence, the church secretary. Florence had worked for the church long before Eric showed up, and more than likely, she would be there long after Eric was gone. Eric often sought her advice on office politics as she had been there long enough to know all the main players and had great relationships with all the other support staff.

Eric willed his body to pivot toward her and plastered a smile on his face. "Yes?"

Florence returned the smile. "Good morning, Pastor Eric. How are you this fine morning?"

Eric paused. This is why he came in the back door. Was God picking on him? "Not bad, Florence. How are you this morning?" *Please don't ask me anything else, Florence. For the love of all that is holy, let me crawl into my office and sit in the darkness.*

"Better than I deserve. Thank you, Pastor Eric," Florence beamed. "It looked like you were in a hurry, so I don't mean to interrupt; however, I was just getting ready to call you. Your 10:00 with Pastor Wheeler has been moved up to 9:30. He had some things come up, so he needs to meet earlier. I checked your calendar, and it appeared that you were open, so I changed your appointment. Is that okay?"

Eric's brain seemed to be stuck in second gear. With Jim's words from yesterday and Christine's resignation letter crowding his thoughts, he was having difficulty making out a clear thought. Eric looked down at his watch. 9:26 A.M. "That's in less than five minutes."

"I know," replied Florence. "That's why I was getting ready to call. Are you available?"

Eric stared blankly at Florence. Everything within him wanted to come up with an adequate reason for not being able to meet with Pastor Wheeler in four minutes. Absolutely nothing came to mind. "Sure, I'll be there in just a few minutes."

With that, Eric turned toward his office, entered, and closed the door. He slumped down in the chair beside the door and closed his eyes.

9:30 A.M. THE CONFRONTATION

Eric walked into Pastor Wheeler's office area. Susan, Pastor Wheeler's secretary, was on the phone, obviously talking to some vendor whose service or product would likely save the church a significant amount of money. Susan was way too polite. It was clear that she was not interested, but she hadn't had the heart to say no earlier in the conversation.

Eric cleared his throat.

Susan looked up and saw him. She covered up the receiver and said in a loud whisper, "Go on in. He's waiting for you."

Eric opened up the office doors and walked in. Pastor Wheeler's office was bathed in nautical decorations. He had paintings of lighthouses, beaches, and stormy seas. On bookshelves, end tables, and his desk, he had replicas of ships, anchors, and compasses. This office was a mariner's haven, and Pastor Wheeler obviously found solace in the sea.

Patrick Wheeler was a fourth generation preacher. His great-great-great-grandfather had come over from Europe and traveled to different congregations on Sundays by horseback. Patrick was called into the ministry at age sixteen and served as the youth pastor of his father's church in Michigan immediately after graduating from seminary. After serving in his father's church for six years, he relocated to central Texas to plant New Hope Community Church. That was fifteen years ago.

Pastor Wheeler was a great bear of a man. At 6' 5", he towered over most men.

Contrary to his impressive size, Patrick was incredibly meek and gentle. He was a terrific communicator, but he rarely opened his mouth unless he had something important to say. He had a contagious smile, and when one was with him, he or she felt like the only one in the room. When he spoke, it was with love and compassion. Everyone felt blessed to have Patrick at the helm of New Hope.

Eric slowly walked toward Patrick's desk and nervously slipped into a chair. Patrick looked up from his desk, smiled, and said "Good morning, Eric." Eric flashed a quick and slightly contrived smile at his boss.

"Good morning, sir."

Patrick proceeded to ask how the wife and kids were, followed by a light-hearted debate over who was going to win Houston a championship first, the Astros or the Texans? Eric was the baseball guy, and Pastor Wheeler was a huge Texan fan.

Eric was totally disarmed. How did Pastor Wheeler do it? He'd be shocked if he didn't already know about Jim, but he didn't let on in the slightest. All pretenses seemed to melt away as Eric felt like he was talking to an old friend, but without warning, Pastor Wheeler brought the conversation back to current affairs.

"So, Eric, how is our children's ministry doing?" Pastor Wheeler asked with a large smile.

Eric's hands were sweating. He wasn't sure why he was so nervous. Just a minute ago they had been talking about sports; now he felt like he was in the hot seat. "Well, Pastor, to be honest, things are a bit rough right now. I have had two key people quit recently. I really don't know what is going on. It seemed like everything was going along just fine, and then all of the sudden *wham*! People are quitting right and left. Totally unexpected. Quite frankly, I'm having a hard time processing everything right now, Pastor."

"Eric, tell me about it. I'd really like to help. Can you tell me what happened yesterday with Jim?"

He wasn't surprised that Pastor Wheeler had already heard about his hallway confrontation. Not much happened at New Hope that didn't get back to Pastor Wheeler. He always had a great pulse on everything that was happening. Eric proceeded to tell him all the gory details. He even shared about his conversation with Jeanne the previous week. "Pastor, I just didn't expect that to happen. I knew I needed to have a conversation with Jim, and he didn't really leave me any other choice."

Pastor Wheeler sat and listened quietly. When Eric finished talking, Pastor Wheeler paused for what seemed like hours. Eric kept thinking, *Come on, just say something.*

"Eric, what do you do that no one else can do?"

Eric looked puzzled. "Excuse me?"

"What can you do that no one else can do?" repeated Pastor Wheeler.

"I can stick out my tongue and touch my nose. Is that what you mean?"

Pastor Wheeler chuckled. "Not exactly. Let me rephrase the question. What is it that you need to do in order for the kids' ministry at our church to be successful?"

"I, well, I guess I have never thought of that before. I don't really know. I guess I run all of New Hope Kids?"

"Well, yes, I suppose that is true, but I was looking for something more specific. Let me ask you this, Eric. If you walked out today and never came back, what would happen to New Hope Kids?"

Eric's eyes got wide. "Am I getting fired?"

Patrick Wheeler startled Eric with a deep belly laugh. "No, Eric. At least, not yet anyway," he said with a wink and a sly smile. "So, what do you think? What would happen if you walked out today?"

"To be honest, I think you'd have a mess on your hands. I think a lot of things would fall apart."

Pastor Wheeler quickly responded, "So, Eric, do you think this is a good thing or a bad thing?"

"Well, I guess it's how you look at it. I'm not trying to toot my own horn, but I'm pretty good at what I do. At least that's what others tell me. So, it would be natural that if I weren't here, things would go downhill quickly. On the other side of things, it just doesn't seem right. It would be a shame to see things fall apart. I've worked very hard to get things to where they are today. I don't know what I'd do differently. Maybe it's just one of those unavoidable things."

Pastor Wheeler removed his glasses and set them on his desk. He folded his hands and leaned forward. "Eric, when was the last time you took your family on vacation? For that matter, when was the last time you attended a church service?"

Eric looked down at his feet. Suddenly he felt ashamed and self-conscious. Either

Pastor Wheeler really wasn't angry about Jim, or he was hiding it well. Regardless, these probing questions hit a nerve with Eric. He thought, *Why all the questions about me? I know I'm not perfect, but what happened yesterday wasn't my fault. Jim was a class-A jerk, and I'm not sure how I feel about being asked all these questions. Why am I on the hot seat?*

"Eric?" Pastor Wheeler questioned.

Eric realized that he hadn't responded. "Sorry, I was just processing your questions. I don't mean any disrespect, but I don't know what all these questions have to do with what happened yesterday."

"Eric, I think they have everything to do with yesterday."

With a confused look on his face, Eric replied reluctantly, "Well, it's been almost two years since I've been on vacation and several months since I attended a service."

Pastor Wheeler paused briefly and asked, "Why do you think that is?"

"Well, it just isn't the same when I am not here; no one does worship or the Bible story the same way I do. The kids love me, Pastor. When I am not here, they can tell, and they miss me. I am gifted to lead and pastor kids. It's not that everything will just fall apart, but things just run better when I'm around."

The next thing pastor Wheeler said made Eric want to vomit.

"Eric, I need you to understand something very important. I didn't hire you to be New Hope Kids. I hired you to lead New Hope Kids."

Eric sat there and stared blankly at the wall just over Pastor Wheeler's shoulder because he couldn't look him in the eye. All kinds of emotions stirred in his chest. He was a little angry that Pastor Wheeler was drilling him this way. He felt like he was getting kicked while he was down. Didn't he understand how humiliating it was to get chewed out by a key volunteer in the middle of the hallway? However, at the same time, there was a voice in the back of his head that agreed with the line of questioning, yet Eric resented it. The questions spoke to his pain. Being the children's pastor at New Hope was the hardest thing he'd ever done. It was like a giant juggling act. It required his constant attention, and he felt that if he missed one Sunday or didn't make that one call then everything might come crashing down. This burden was heavy, and it was affecting Eric. Although they didn't really talk about it, this burden was affecting his family as well. This was a really sensitive area for him and Eric wasn't exactly sure he was comfortable talking about it in this way. Pastor Wheeler was probably the person he'd go to, but on his terms and his time, not like this.

To Eric's dismay, Pastor Wheeler continued. "I fear that you've created a culture in our children's ministry that doesn't reflect me or the values this church is based on. New Hope has always been about teamwork and collaboration, and I'm not sure that's the way you've been leading."

Pastor Wheeler paused for a few seconds. "Eric, I talked to both Jim and Christine last night."

"You called them? What did Christine tell you?"

Pastor Wheeler held his hand up, "No, I didn't call anyone. Eric, you're my children's pastor, and I'm behind you. They called me, and I heard them out. I told them that they needed to go to you. I'll be honest with you though. I think they're on to something. I'm not saying that I agree with what either of them did. I think that Jim's behavior what out of line, and Christine called me after she emailed you her resignation, which I thought was tacky; and I told her that. However, they both had serious concerns, and I tend to agree with the pattern that they're both pointing to. It seems to me that the time has come for you to raise leaders and develop some teams that are equipped to get the job done with or without you."

Eric slumped down in his chair and stared blankly at the desk in front of him. He knew his pastor was right, but that didn't change the fact that he was angry. He wasn't sure if he was angry because of the way this was all going down or because he had let people, more specifically, Pastor Wheeler down. Eric had always been successful, and it was painful to hear that he had failed in this area.

Pastor Wheeler stood up and walked around his desk and sat in the chair beside Eric. He turned the chair to face Eric. "I hadn't planned to deal with all this stuff with you today, but it's probably good it happened. I've got some big news to share with you, and it's going to have a pretty big impact on our children's ministry."

Eric perked up a little and turned to face his pastor.

"You know we've been in a season of growth, which is both exciting and challenging. Looking at the last several years of attendance data, we know that we spike in attendance for non-holiday weekends a few weeks after Easter. If trends continue like they have in past years, we're going to be out of room this year, and we have to make space for our families."

Eric wasn't sure he liked where this was going.

"The board has been discussing this now for the past three weeks, and we're all con-fident that New Hope needs to begin Saturday-night services on Easter weekend."

"Are you serious?" Eric blurted out before he had time to think.

Pastor Wheeler smiled at Eric's blunder. "Serious as a heart attack. I get it—no one really wants to give up Saturday nights, but we really don't see any other option. We're out of space, and I never want New Hope to turn someone away because there aren't enough seats."

Eric started to get a little worked up. "What about another service on Sunday? Has anyone considered that at all?"

"Yes, we've looked at several options, and we all feel that Saturday is our best option to increase space."

"Have you and the board considered how hard this is going to be on the children's ministry? Do you know how hard it is to get volunteers, much less to have volunteers show up to serve on a Saturday night?"

Pastor Wheeler answered calmly, "Eric, we're 100 percent behind you. Yes, we have discussed how difficult this is going to be for much of the staff and their teams. However, we're moving forward with what's best for our church and our community. You're not alone in this. We're all in this, man."

Eric wasn't happy. At the moment he could only process how this new information was ruining everything. He knew that in the next few weeks, he would have to start ramping up his planning for summer camp and the special activities he'd been thinking about. With a Saturday service, it was going to be a lot harder to find the time to do all that.

Pastor Wheeler adjusted his chair and leaned in a little more. "Eric, you've had a lot dumped on in the last twenty-four hours. Honestly, you've had a lot dumped on you in the past twenty minutes. I need you to take some time to process this change. The stuff we talked about concerning raising leaders and building teams, you're going to have to truly carry that out in order to make Saturday night services successful. You can't do this alone, nor do I expect you to. Just promise me that you're going to take some time and pray about all of this. Ask God to prepare your heart for what needs to be done and to prepare the heart of those who will join your Saturday teams."

Eric slumped into his chair again. He was utterly defeated. He felt like a failure that had just been told to climb an un-climbable mountain. His day was getting worse by the minute.

Pastor Wheeler put his hand on Eric's shoulder. He paused a long time before saying, "I know that this is a lot for you to take in. Honestly, it's probably the last thing you want to hear right now. I know what you've been through. I've been there. Anyone who's been in ministry for any amount of time develops a few battle scars. Please hear me, Eric, I'm really sorry about what happened yesterday, I truly am; however, I think that it might have happened for a reason. It could be exactly what needed to happen in your life to prepare you for the season ahead. Consider it a wake-up call or a catalyst for change. I believe in you, and I believe that you've got what it takes to get the job done. I really do."

Eric knew that his pastor meant well. He was kind man and a great pastor, but Eric wasn't listening anymore. All Eric could hear were the thoughts screaming in his head: *Rebecca's going to be so mad. She's already on my case as it is about working too much. Now I've got to give up Saturdays. Let's be honest, I'm not going to be giving up Saturday nights; it's going to take most of the day.*

His thoughts took a darker tone. *Pastor Wheeler and his board really aren't seeing reality. None of them have been children's pastors. Pastor Wheeler was only a student pastor before planting New Hope. They have no idea how much work it takes for a children's ministry to pull off a service, much less a Saturday-night service.*

Eric's thoughts were ugly, but they were honest. At that point he couldn't wait to be out of that meeting.

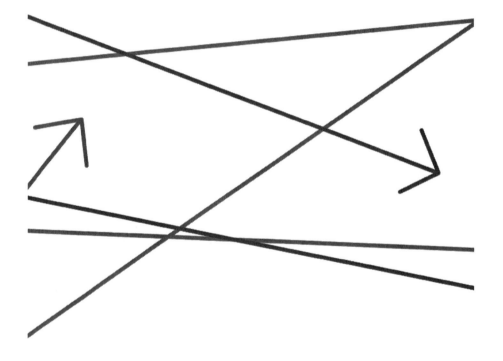

Chapter 2:
Leadership Under Authority

DEANA HAYES

I remember the first day on the job like it was yesterday. I strolled into the church building not really knowing what to expect. The senior pastor greeted me with some warm and welcoming words, and then he escorted me to my office and asked that I meet with him in his office in a few minutes. The first thing I noticed was that my office had windows, a supposed luxury in the world of kidmin, so I knew things were already off to a good start. After setting some personal things down and again admiring the view from my window, I strolled down the hall to meet with my senior pastor. We went over the typical personnel and administrative stuff—those fun yet necessary tax and insurance forms. And afterward, he sent me to my office to begin my job.

I was so excited to get things going in children's ministry at this church. I was the first children's pastor my church had ever hired. It was a new venture, and I was eager to do a great job. Isn't that what we all desire—to be the best at what we do? We attend school and conferences, and we network with others to be the best at our job. We dream of new and better programs that will reach more and more kids. We seek to acquire the newest tools and resources so that we can be the best (not in a conceited way, of course). We're passionate about what we've been called to do, and we quickly become absorbed in this huge and complex world of our vision for ministry. Sounds familiar, doesn't it?

Well, did I have a lot to learn.

Having a huge vision for children's ministry isn't wrong. Actually, it's essential. But one of the biggest and most important things I have learned is the importance of knowing the vision of the house and submitting to my senior or lead pastor. To submit means to yield oneself to the will or authority of another. More personally, to submit as a children's pastor means to know my senior pastor's heart. Where is God leading him for the congregation in which we both serve? It is crucial to our personal well being as well as the success of our church to know that vision. Mark 3:24-26 says, "If a kingdom is divided against itself, that kingdom cannot stand. If a house is divided against itself, that house cannot stand. And if Satan opposes himself and is divided, he cannot stand; his end has come."

Naturally, as children's pastors, we may wonder, how exactly do I serve my senior leader? or why do I put his calling before my own? Well the why is an easy one to answer. The relationship between a senior pastor and his associate pastors is often the key to the health and ministry of a church. Although we may have been hired because of our vision for the children's ministry and our stated expectation is to lead the children's ministry, our top priority must always be to assist the pastor in his vision for the church. Period.

I have often heard children's ministers argue, "But I went to school to serve the local church as the children's pastor," or "I was hired as the children's pastor; therefore, my job is to lead and oversee the ministry to children, so what does getting to know the vision of the house or serving my senior pastor have do with my key responsibilities?"

Well, everything.

When the local church hires a person to oversee any area of ministry, what they are actually doing is hiring an associate to the pastor. The church is hiring an associate pastor who will assist the senior pastor in moving the church to accomplish the vision God gave him for that particular church. Once on staff, the senior pastor will delegate authority to the associate in overseeing and leading a ministry in a specific area. In our cases, that specific area happens to be a vibrant ministry to children. Therefore, it is not your ministry; it's an extension of the ministries offered by your local church. Let me say that again. It is not YOUR ministry. Sometimes I think that we get that confused. Plainly said, you have been entrusted to lead that area of ministry in the way it should go in line with the vision of the house. Our work should reflect highly on our senior pastors. Remember, we were hired to serve our senior pastor and his vision for the church, not the other way around.

Why did I have to learn this the hard way? I got to the point where I wanted the church to grow so badly that I was very eager to do something, anything, to move it forward. I failed to listen to my senior pastor. I did not honor him, nor did I extend the respect that he deserved as an ordained man of God. I had my own ideas of what could be done, and I knew they were great ideas.

Don't get me wrong, having a desire, in and of itself, to grow and move a church is not wrong, but the way we try to see it through may have its faults. We must be careful in how we build and direct the ministry we've been given authority to lead. Building a ministry to children that teaches, encourages, challenges, strengthens, and leads children to the throne of grace for our own success is wrong. Reaching out to equip families, encourage moms, and develop dads in spite of what our leadership has asked us to do is failure. The ends never justify the means. In all that we do, we must build our ministry to children in a way that aligns with and reflects the vision of the house.

It is so easy to sit in our offices and totally get lost within our own ministry. Praying for, planning, and dreaming of what to do next are consuming. We wonder how we can improve our safety and security system in a way that gives parents more confidence? What tools can we seek or develop to better train and equip our staff? Which conferences should we attend to grow in both faith and skills, learn from great communicators, and network with other like-minded pastors?

As a children's minister, there's always more to do than we'll have time for. There's more to think about than we'll have time to actually think about it. There's nothing wrong with all of these things, right? This is what we were hired to do, isn't it?

Stop. Get up from your desk. Walk out of your office, and go join a co-worker in his or her office. Ask him or her about plans he or she has for the ministry he or she has authority to lead. Probe deeper. Ask questions. How does what this person is talking about intersect with the children's ministry? How can you help him or her be successful? How can he or she help you to be successful? Are you both headed in the same direction, following the vision your pastor laid out for your church?

We have a tendency to isolate ourselves in our own world and ministry, and we forget our place. We're on a team. We're working together. We are working for our senior pastor. We must not forget this.

Think of how much easier it's going to be for our senior pastors to lead the church if everyone who works for him is putting his needs, dreams, and desires first. The church is looking at him to lead the vision to fruition. We must take some time to help him.

In order to truly help our senior pastors and to fulfill our roles as associate pastors, we must get to know them. How can we keep the vision for the church before our volunteers if we don't know what it is? How can we lead others to help the church fulfill what it was placed on this earth to do if we don't know what makes our senior leader's heart beat? This only comes with time spent getting to know him both professionally and personally.

As I look at past actions, I see that this is another area in which I failed my first senior pastor. I did not take the time to get to know him on a personal level. I never talked about how I could lead with him and not build something separate from him. I wish I knew then what I know now.

So, what does this look like practically? Where does one even begin? Actually, it's not that hard. If we're going to truly serve our pastors, we need to get to know our pastors. We can't even begin to support our leaders until we know what's truly important in his or her heart, so we begin by truly getting to know him or her.

There are some ridiculously easy ways to begin that most seem to overlook. Some pastors blog. If my pastor blogs, I read it—every post. There's no quicker way to our pastors' passion than through a blog. Other pastors read. If my pastor is an avid reader, I find out his favorite book, and I read it. This may seem obvious, but we can also learn a lot through listening. When I attend church services, I listen and hear my pastor's heart. And when I miss, I make sure to listen to the sermon later that week.

Next, we can begin taking initiative and start seeking our pastors out. For example, we can schedule lunch appointments or a meeting for any time he or she has available. A great way to reach out is to bring his or her favorite coffee along and then take advantage of the opportunity by asking questions that matter:

- How were you called into ministry?
- What do you know now that you wish you knew then?
- What has been the greatest victory you've experienced in ministry?
- What has been the hardest thing you've had to do in ministry?
- What ministry book has impacted you more than any other?
- What's your dream for this church?

- What can I take off your plate (e.g., hospital visits, counseling appointments, or even teaching from time to time)?
- How can my ministry better reflect what you want to see come to pass in the church?

A prepared children's minister doesn't just show up for meetings. He or she comes with a list of questions. In fact, a prepared minister has questions ready at anytime, so even if there's a quick impromptu meeting in the car while driving to an off-site meeting or running into each other in the parking lot after a Sunday service, we can be prepared. When we seek our pastors out in these ways, we will hear his or her heart, and we will know how to pray for him or her. We will clearly understand the vision and values that need to become our vision and values. This isn't just advice for beginners. This needs to be a way of life.

As we continue to develop a strong relationship with our pastors, serving his or her vision will become natural. Because we carry our pastors' visions and values, we'll do anything to help see them come to pass. We'll become much more intentional about helping him or her be successful. We'll also get to a point where we welcome input into our ministry plans, and we'll begin to look for ways we can align our gifts where our senior pastors may not be as strong.

More often than not, kids' pastors operate their ministries in spite of their senior pastors. Whether it is true or not, they see their pastor as a hindrance or obstacle to overcome or work around. They might complain by saying, "My pastor just doesn't 'get' the importance of kidmin," or they'll say, "No one values the kids at this church!" Although this perception may be true, it is backward thinking. It assumes the perspective that the senior pastor exists to serve the children's ministry. Remember, we were hired to serve our pastor and his or her vision, not the other way around.

But what about the kids? If they aren't our top priority, then won't they fall through the cracks? Isn't that what we're called to—to fight for them and their spiritual condition? That's a really great question. Concern for the kids and fighting for them is a noble gesture but not at the expense of contributing to a healthy relationship with the staff and pastor. That only breeds dysfunction and silos in ministry.

When a children's pastor (or any pastor for that matter) begins to serve his or her pastor, he sets a significant precedent. He plays out a model of what service should look like in that church. In the same way that the kids' pastor puts making his or her pastor successful, his or her staff and key leaders learn to do the same. What would ministry look like if the key leaders who lead under us wanted to make us successful and serve our visions as their top priorities? That would be pretty amazing, wouldn't it? Well, when we model that type of behavior, it's not that far of a stretch to expect that from our teams as well. That's the picture of healthy, self-less ministry where others' needs are put before our own, and God has a way of taking care of what's important to us.

Let's look at what Scripture say about this approach to ministry leadership: "Be shepherds of God's flock that is under your care, watching over them—not because you must, but because you are willing, as God wants you to be; not pursuing dishonest gain, but eager to serve" (1 Peter 5:2). This is a serious command and responsibility that our pastors must wear personally. It's what God has called them to do, and they will be held accountable to how well they shepherded God's flock. We have to remember our part. We are co-shepherds, helping our pastor successfully do what he or she is called to do. Our pastors need for us to do our part. They're depending on us. How much more can we bless them when we truly lay down our desires to see them succeed? I believe that God honors that kind of approach.

"If they were all one part, where would the body be? As it is, there are many parts, but one body. The eye cannot say to the hand, 'I don't need you!' And the head cannot say to the feet, 'I don't need you!'" (1 Cor.12:19-21). Although seldom said, many church staff members have at least thought these very things about other staff members. Too many kids' pastors posture themselves this way in relation to their senior leadership. Their actions communicate, "I don't need you. Just preach to the adults, and make sure I have a budget, and I'll be fine on my own."

Too often we allow our call to children's ministry to trump our responsibility to serve senior leadership. We have it in our head that doing our own thing is okay. We might even pull the God-card and say that we're just being obedient to our calling even though in our hearts we know that this kind of dysfunction brings little glory to Jesus. Regardless of how we feel about our pastor or his thoughts and values about children's ministry, there is a responsibility on us to live out 1 Corinthians 12:19-21. Our pastors have a heavy burden, and even if they're not leading out this way like they should, we can initiate biblical unity.

Let's play this out a little: What if you were the agent of change in your church? What if you put some of your dreams and your vision temporarily on hold and you decided to commit the next six months to truly serving your pastor in a humbling and sacrificial way? Do you think it might change the dynamic in your relationship with the pastor? Do you think it could change the culture on your staff? What about when it comes to the area you serve? When your pastor feels that you are 110 percent behind him, do you think he'll help you get what your ministry needs in order to be successful? Probably more so than if your ministry was segmented and self-serving. After six months of leading this way, don't you think it might have an impact on your local congregation? So what's the harm in giving this a shot?

One of my favorite verses is found in Isaiah 11:6:

> *The wolf will live with the lamb,*
> *the leopard will lie down with the goat,*
> *the calf and the lion and the yearling together;*
>
> *and a little child will lead them.*

I know that the context and message of this verse is different, but what if this were truly a picture of what could happen to our church staff? I have certainly served with some staff that could be described as wolves. I've even served with a goat or two. I've seen staff dynamics that looked more like a variety of zoo animals all thrown in the same cage. But what if the pastor of children led staff change in this way? That would be pretty satisfying, wouldn't it? It would be something that Christ would have done. I imagine it is something He would be pleased with as well since He has a soft spot in His heart for the church.

I didn't get this right to begin with. I learned the hard way—the way so many of us do. I now serve a different senior pastor and do all that I can to support him in leading our church in the way he feels God intends. It isn't always easy, but I feel I'm getting it right more often than not. It is a joy to lead a ministry knowing it beats to the same drum as the other ministries in my church. That's the way ministry was always supposed to be—in sync with senior leadership.

Your Eric Trap

Don't fall into the same trap as Eric. Go beyond reading inspirational words and stories, and measure your life and ministry against the traps many in ministry fall into as did Eric. Open up your journal or notebook, and take time to answer the questions below. Allow the principles in this chapter to translate into the context of your life and ministry.

From memory, write out the mission/vision of your church.

Now, give yourself a score from 1-5.

1 - I have no idea what the vision is.

2 - I don't know it, but I kind of paraphrased it.

3 - I pretty much know it word for word, but it has little impact on my day-to-day work.

4 - I keep the vision in mind when planning events and programs, but long periods of time go by without giving the vision much thought.

5 - Not a day goes by when I don't read or recite the vision. It comes up regularly in conversation. My staff and volunteers all know the vision intimately.

Schedule a meeting with your senior pastor. Share with him or her how you answered the above questions. Discuss the vision and how you can better lead your ministry toward the vision.

Identify which areas within your ministry do not totally align with the vision of your church. Which areas need to be adjusted? Which areas need to be eliminated?

List three things you can begin doing that will help you to better serve your pastor. Assign dates to those three things.

Where is their disunity on your staff team? What is causing it? What can you do to fix it?

Tuesday

MONDAY, FEBRUARY 18TH, 11:28 A.M. (THE DAY BEFORE)

Following his meeting with Pastor Wheeler, Eric crept back to his office and locked the door behind him. He turned out the lights and sat in his chair. Too much had happened to him, and he needed time to process.

After almost two hours of silence, Eric got himself to a place where he could at least begin to think about getting some work done. As far the issues with Jim and Christine, he was beginning to see things from Pastor Wheeler's point of view. When he was completely honest with himself, he admitted that things hadn't been adding up for a long time. He became a children's pastor because he was really good with kids and felt that God was calling him to this work. As a children's pastor, he made sure that he was closely connected to everything involving the kids. He thought that was what he was expected to do, but he felt the tension that came with growth—it was getting harder and harder to be everywhere, and Eric knew he was wearing out.

Pastor Wheeler's challenge and encouragement opened a whole new world to Eric, but he wasn't exactly sure how he felt about it. He never really saw team building and developing leaders as a primary job function. Although it made a lot of sense, it scared him to try something totally out of his comfort zone. Regardless, Eric resolved that he was willing to learn if that's what it required.

The bigger problem facing Eric was figuring out how to recruit a team for the new Saturday-night service—the mere thought of those three words sent a shiver down his spine. He struggled between his genuine love and appreciation for Pastor Wheeler and his resentment from having all of this responsibility dumped on him.

Eric felt that if Pastor Wheeler understood more about what it was really like to lead a children's ministry, he would have at least included Eric in the decision-making process.

A knock at his door startled Eric back to reality.

He jumped up and headed toward the door. Fumbling in the dark office, nearly tripping on a basketball and pool noodles he used for an object lesson three weeks ago, he reached out for the light switch and flipped it on before unlocking the door. He opened the door quickly and found himself inches away from a frowning Florence.

"Pastor Eric, is everything okay?"

"Yeah, yeah. I'm fine," Eric quickly said with the biggest plastic smile he could muster. "Sorry, it's just been a rough morning, and I was collecting my thoughts."

The wrinkles between Florence's eyes sank a little deeper.

Eric felt his cheeks turn red and forced a coughing laugh. "I'm sorry, Florence. A little grace please, I've just not been myself today."

Florence softened, "Oh, don't worry. That's fine, I was just concerned for you. That's all. Listen, I was trying to track you down because I just got a call from Stephanie Haynes. She said she has sent you a few emails and left a few voice messages, yet she hasn't heard anything back from you. She just wanted to confirm that you were still available for lunch tomorrow with her and her husband."

Eric closed his eyes and thought for a second. "Yes. Yes, I'm supposed to have lunch with them, but I thought that was on the nineteenth."

Florence's brow wrinkled again, "Tomorrow is the nineteenth."

"Oh, right," Eric said and subconsciously rubbed his hands through his hair. This was probably one of the worst weeks for lunch with the Haynes, but he had no way of knowing that when he scheduled it a week ago. "Would you mind calling her back for me and letting her know that we're still good for tomorrow?"

"I'd be glad to," Florence said as she turned to return to her desk. She paused for a second and turned back. "Are you sure you're okay? Is there anything I can do?"

"I'm fine, Florence. Thank you though. I'll make it," Eric said with a weak smile as he closed the door.

TUESDAY, FEBRUARY 19TH, 12:07 P.M.

Eric sped down Airport Drive, late for his lunch appointment with Greg and Stephanie. He'd gotten caught up in e-mails at the office and totally lost track of time. It was actually Florence who pushed him out the door. She knew Eric too well.

The day before had gotten a little better as it went on. He had gotten some work done and spent more than an hour on the phone with Christine. He had given her an opportunity to share her frustrations that led to her resignation e-mail. It had been tough to hear, and if it hadn't been for his talk with Pastor Wheeler earlier that morning, he probably would have gotten really defensive. Whether it was wisdom gained from experience or he was just too broken down from the events of the previous twenty-four hours, he had just let her talk. Eric had decided to take a risk and had honestly shared with her the conversation he and Pastor Wheeler had had earlier that morning. He apologized for the way he hadn't been leading, and something surprising had happened. She rescinded her resignation, sort of. She explained that things hadn't been healthy, but she was willing to work with someone who could be authentic about shortcomings. She wanted to get more involved in her small group, but she offered to totally own early childhood for the future Saturday-night services. This had been a very bright spot in an otherwise dark and dreary day. Eric knew that he needed to have a similar conversation with Jim, but he didn't expect things to go the same way.

Eric had decided not to tell Rebecca about Saturday-night services yet. Sunday and Monday had been hard enough. For the past few months, Rebecca had constantly been on his case about the hours he was putting in. It had been several weeks since they had had any quality time together as a couple or as a family. No matter how he brought it up, she wasn't going to take it well; and he knew he only had a few days to tell her before she found out from someone else, which would be really bad. Eric had to come up with a plan for how he would both pastor Saturday services and make more time for his family. The math looked impossible, but he had to have some semblance of a plan before dropping the bomb on Rebecca.

Eric switched to the turn lane and pulled into the Olive Garden parking lot. *Ten minutes late, that's not too bad*, Eric thought to himself. Eric replayed in his head the chance meeting that had spurred on this lunch date.

The previous Wednesday he had run into Stephanie Haynes in the church hallway. She and her husband Greg were always so verbally complimentary to Eric as the children's pastor. When he had seen her in his peripheral while cleaning out a hall closet, he had made sure to turn and greet her. She had mentioned she was on the way to women's Bible study; but she was glad she ran into him because she and her husband had some things they had wanted to talk to Eric about concerning their seven-year-old son. Then she had offered for her and her husband to treat Eric to lunch the following week. Eric, very fond of their little boy Gregory, had been more than happy to agree to meet with them.

As Eric walked into the restaurant, he began to wonder what it was about Gregory that they were concerned about. Eric found the Haynes at their table; and they exchanged greetings, shook hands, and commenced with small talk catching up on how their families were doing. After they ordered their lunch, Eric put his elbows on the table and got right to the point.

"Well, thank you for inviting me to lunch. It's always good to spend time with you, but I know you had a reason for our meeting today. What can I help you with?"

Stephanie began, "Eric, we're just so thankful that you took time out of your week to meet with us. We both know how incredibly busy you must be."

"No problem, guys. That's why I'm here."

"So, I guess we'll get to the point. We absolutely love New Hope, and we've been so happy since we came last October. I've really enjoyed the Bible study I'm in, and when he's not traveling, Greg has enjoyed the men's Thursday-morning gatherings. More importantly, Gregory absolutely loves you! I know you've got so many kids that you pastor, but Gregory hangs on to every word you say. On the car ride home, he tells us everything, and I mean everything: he tells us the Bible story, what songs you all sang, the games you played, as well as, the silly skit character you played that week. You really are making an impression, and we're very thankful for that."

Eric beamed. "I can't even begin to tell you how much that means to me. I love the kids of New Hope, and I often feel like the luckiest guy in the world to get paid to do what I do, but hearing what you just said is so encouraging. You wouldn't believe the week I've had, so this is good news."

Greg smiled, "Won't believe the week you've had? It's only Tuesday."

Eric laughed out loud. "Yeah, I know. It's been that bad!" He cleared his throat and continued, "Well, thank you for the compliments, but I'm sure you didn't bring me to lunch just to tell me all that."

Greg jumped in, "No, we didn't. We're grateful for all you've done for Gregory, but we're concerned that what Gregory is getting isn't enough. Neither Stephanie nor I grew up in Christian homes, so we don't have any example to point to. Although we feel that Gregory's getting a great church experience with you, we just don't believe that it's enough. It doesn't take a lot of common sense to see that one hour a week probably isn't enough to ensure Gregory is going to know what he needs to know when it comes to being a Christian."

Eric wasn't exactly sure where Greg was going with this.

Stephanie spoke up. "Greg and I have been talking about this a lot lately. Gregory spends seven hours in school five days a week: thirty minutes every day practicing the piano; two to four hours every week playing soccer; and he'd probably play video games all the time if we let him. But when it comes to church, something we feel is more important than all of these things, he's only there one hour a week. He has his little Bible, and he reads it most days, thanks to your constant encouragement; however, it just doesn't all seem to add up. If we want the faith he has as a boy to be something he takes with him as an adult, it seems like he needs more than just an hour a week."

Greg joined in, "We really feel this is important. We're willing to do just about anything."

Eric grinned from ear to ear. "Wow, this is great! I'm thrilled you're so concerned about Gregory's spiritual life. He's lucky to have parents who care so much."

"Don't you get asked this by other parents? Certainly we're not the only ones?" Stephanie asked.

"You'd be surprised, Stephanie."

Eric leaned back and crossed his arms. "Parents love their kids, but most don't have a clue when it comes to their kids' spiritual lives. I know it's not that they don't care; it's just that maybe they don't know to care. Does that make sense?"

Greg shrugged, "Well, I can't speak for any other parents. Like we said, we're new at this, and we want the best for Gregory. We want him to have what we didn't. What do you suggest?"

"Well, I see that we have lots of options, but first, I want to encourage you to do what you've been doing. Keep supporting his faith development like you have. You guys bring him to church every week, and that's so important. So many people today are so inconsistent in coming to church. It used to be that most people attended every other week, but now it seems that most people come less often than that. If you want him to really get this stuff and make it stick, he needs to have the kind of consistency that you've already been providing him.

"Do you know anything about our Wednesday night program for elementary kids?" Eric asked.

"Not really," replied Greg. "We've not really considered Wednesday night as an option because it doesn't end until 8:30, and we usually have Gregory in bed by eight. We live a good ten miles from New Hope, so if we came, we wouldn't be able to have the little guy in bed until after nine."

Stephanie put her hand on Greg's and looked at Eric, "Well, tell us what it's about.

We're pretty strict about Gregory's bed time, but we're open to negotiation."
Stephanie winked at Greg.

"Alright, Eric," Greg conceded, "I'm open to the possibility . . . maybe. Sell me on it,
and we'll see."

Eric smiled as he leaned in, "Well, I'm not suggesting you rearrange your whole
schedule or anything, but I'm just letting you know what we offer. I know this is
important to you, and I do feel that what we offer on Wednesday nights can help
Gregory take deeper steps in his faith."

"Sounds great." Stephanie smiled. "What's it like?"

"Well, it's a great program I have developed over the last two years. I've tried a lot
of different curriculum but ended up writing something myself that better fit our
kids. Essentially, the kids come in at 7:30, and we spend the first 20-30 minutes
getting all their wiggles out. We spend time on the playground or on the front field
playing games. Once they've hit the bathrooms, washed their hands, and gotten a
drink, we come in for the good stuff. For the next thirty minutes, we pretty much
have a Bible study for kids. Although we will cover a variety of topics over the year,
I take the time to teach them how to use their Bibles, how to find things using a
concordance, and other Bible-study tools. My main objective in our Wednesday
night program is to help introduce kids to the Bible and help them fall in love with
God's Word. I feel that if they can get that, then they'll have that the rest of their
lives. We spend the last 20-30 minutes singing a few songs, praying for each other,
and working on memory verses."

"That sounds fantastic!" Stephanie erupted. "I don't love the idea of Gregory being
up that late, and I think I'll dread Thursday mornings, but I can't imagine him
missing an experience like that."

"I agree," Eric replied, a little proud of himself. He had worked really hard to develop his Wednesday program. From the feedback he'd received so far, the kids really liked it, and the parents *loved* it.

"Honestly," Eric said, "it's all about discipleship. Sunday mornings are great, but it's not discipleship. Wednesday nights are really all about developing Gregory to be able to stand on his own feet when it comes to his faith. Think about it for a second. Stephanie, you have your small group, the women's Bible study, right? Greg, you meet with a group of men most Thursdays. Why shouldn't Gregory have that same experience? Kids aren't that different from adults in spiritual matters. Plus, we're still shaping the bigger picture of discipleship for kids at New Hope. I have big plans for the future. For kids involved on Wednesday nights, I'm thinking of developing a weekend retreat every semester next year, and maybe, in a few years, we'll even create a mission-trip experience for graduating fifth graders. Cool, huh?"

"Eric, I must admit. I'm impressed." Greg stuck his hand out across the table. "You sold me. Actually, I'll let Stephanie make the decision as she's the one who gets Gregory up in the mornings, but it sound's like she's willing to be flexible."

"It's a compromise that I'm willing to make. Eric, it sounds like the program is wonderful, and I'm sure that Gregory is going to love it. Honestly, you're such a hero to him, and we love your influence on him," said Stephanie.

"Stephanie, Greg, I'm honored. I'm going to love having Gregory with me on Wednesday nights. I can promise you that not only is he going to love it, but it will shape his life and equip him to be a lifelong follower of Jesus."

Eric leaned back in his chair, "You know, we're going to have some other opportunities down the road as well. This year I'm planning to start a summer camp for our elementary kids. You want to talk about life-change, wait until they've been away from home for four days and 100 percent focused on God's plan for them."

"That's great! I loved camp when I was a kid." Greg smiled. "Of course, it was just boy-scout camp where we learned archery, canoeing, and all that other woodsy stuff. Will your camp be like that?"

"Sort of, but not really. We will pack in all the fun things about going to camp like swimming, campfires, hiking, and games; but we'll also spend a lot of time focusing on the kids' relationships with God." Eric leaned in and put his elbows on the table, "I'm telling you, think of the impact. For most of the kids who come to New Hope, they only spend 20-40 hours a year at church, depending on how often they come. However, at camp, I'll have practically twice as many hours in just a few days. Can you imagine the difference I can make in the lives of these kids if I have that much concentrated time?

"I hope you see how passionate I am about this. Our time is very limited. These kids will grow up in no time, and right now is the time to make the biggest impact." Eric smiled, "I'll do just about anything short of sin to reach these kids."

Stephanie reached over and grabbed Greg's hand, "Eric, your passion is obvious, and we're glad we ended up at New Hope, even if it's just for Gregory's sake." She looked at Greg, "Isn't that right, honey?"

Greg smiled shyly, "Absolutely, dear. Absolutely." Greg turned his attention back to Eric. "So, what else, Eric? Gregory is in Kids Church every Sunday, and starting this, week he'll be in Kid's Church on Wednesday nights. I don't see any reason why he won't attend summer camp either as well as whatever else you might add."

He paused for a second. "Is there anything else that we should be doing? Stephanie and I are still kind of new at this whole faith thing, but we figure that there is probably something we can do beyond just dropping him off. Again, we're grateful that you're providing so much, but, certainly, there has to be something else we can do."

Eric replied without missing a beat. "Sure, there are several things you can do. Obviously parents play a pretty big role in their kids' lives. It's just that a lot of parents are not always equipped to lead their kids spiritually. Unfortunately, like I mentioned earlier, most parents don't even seem all that interested, so that's why I work so hard to provide what we do at New Hope. I feel a heavy responsibility for every kid that walks into our building, and I want New Hope to be a place where every kid is reached and equipped. Do you guys get the take-home cards on Sundays?"

Greg replied with a sly grin, "You mean the multicolored-paper forest growing in the backseat floorboards of my car?"

Stephanie playfully slapped Greg's hand, "Greg, don't be like that. He doesn't want to hear about that." Stephanie turned to Eric, "I'm so sorry. I'm sure you probably put a lot of work into those papers; they just don't seem to make it out of the car."

"Ha! No worries. You're not hurting my feelings. At least your papers make it to the car. Most don't survive the parking lot." Eric laughed.

"On a serious note, though, you could try to use the take-home sheet. You might want to grab it from Gregory when you pick him up from Kids Church. On the take-home sheet there are a lot of activities that he can do throughout the week that will reinforce what we teach on Sunday. There is a place where you can sign that he's done all the extra work. If he brings the sheet back the following week, he will win a prize. It's a really great way for parents to see what their kids are learning and to encourage their kids to continue the lesson."

Eric leaned back and crossed his arms with a matter-of-fact look on his face. "You know what? I have another idea of something you could do."

1:14 P.M. A SMALL VICTORY

It was an eleven-minute drive to the church office from the restaurant. Seven traffic lights, two exits down the interstate, and one school zone. Eric seemed to drive the entire route from some preprogrammed area of his brain. The smile on Eric's face remained the entire drive back to the office. This lunch appointment with the Haynes was the silver lining on his less-than-spectacular week.

At first, Eric was a little surprised at himself. He had never been the kind of guy to just put it all out there like he did with Greg and Stephanie, but the timing seemed to be just right and instinct had kicked in. The Haynes seemed to genuinely want to know how to be better parents when it came to spiritual matters, and Eric simply suggested that if they served in Kids Church, they'd know more about what Gregory was learning, and they'd learn some of the techniques of teaching faith to a child, namely their own child. So next month the Haynes were going to join the 9:00 o'clock service's elementary team.

Eric pulled into the church parking lot and took a deep breath. It had been a rough week, but Eric was enjoying this little victory. He smiled to himself as he thought, *I can't wait to tell the gang about this tomorrow.*

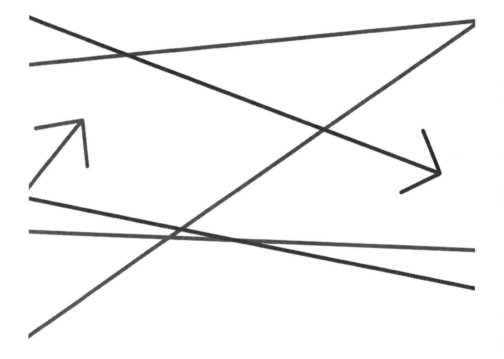

Chapter 3:
Activate Parental Leadership

SHERRI EPPERSON

When my husband and I became parents, we didn't know much about parenting. As a teacher, I had a lot of experience working with parents, and I was well adept to leading and teaching children, but being a parent was a completely different experience. What surprised my husband and I the most was the lack of instructions parents are given when leaving the hospital, or, in our case, the adoption agency. When we've bought a TV, refrigerator, or some other appliance from the store, we've typically been given a thick instruction manual detailing the care and maintenance of each of our new appliances. These owners' manuals even include a pretty robust troubleshooting guide for when we experience problems. But when we were going home with a precious child, we were sent off with a few pointers, a bunch of congratulations, and a few balloons. We quickly realized that we were far from prepared.

In the first few weeks, we were grateful for family and friends who stopped by to check in on us. I'm not sure what would have happened without their help. They gave us advice on all the things we had questions about. Eventually, we became more confident as parents because we felt equipped to do the task of raising children. Looking back, we're proud of how our kids have grown up healthy and whole.

Many years of working in family ministry have helped me to see a similar lack of parental preparation when it comes to raising kids spiritually. If parents aren't really given thorough instructions on raising their kids physically, a guide to spiritual development may not even enter a parent's thinking. Physical development is very tangible and commands a parent's attention where spiritual needs are often unseen, so parents tend to give little attention to their kids' spiritual development.

This is where the church is supposed to step in, right? My experience has shown me that the modern church has stepped in to help parents develop children spiritually, but often, it's not in a healthy way that promotes long-term spiritual growth. For years the church has said to parents, "Bring your kids to our exciting programs, and we'll teach them everything they need to know. You just go to your service, and we'll take care of the kids. We're the experts in this kind of stuff." And parents have gladly relinquished control of spiritual development to the church. It seems like a great arrangement, but studies and experience are showing that this method isn't really working.

What helped my husband and I become great parents were the advice and help of friends and family. They'd stop by and give us some ideas to try, or they would call to encourage us to stay strong and keep doing what we were doing. They didn't do it for us. We didn't relinquish the responsibility of physically meeting our kids' needs to someone else, except for the occasional night out. What made us successful and helped us raise healthy kids is that we were empowered and equipped to do it ourselves. The same is true of spiritual development. True success is seen when the church empowers and equips parents to lead the spiritual development of their kids.

As a ministry leader, we need to understand our role in the spiritual development of kids. We provide an incredible secondary voice in the life of a child. Although many families do nothing and, as children's ministers, our secondary influence often is their only spiritual guidance, we must not forget that a parent at the helm of spiritual development will always trump the church at the helm. We can offer evangelism and discipleship program five days a week, but our influence will never be as great as that of a mom engaging with her daughter over spiritual matters.

The most eloquent children's sermon with perfectly timed illustrations and thorough small-group time will never compare to the nightly bedtime prayer shared between a father and a son.

So where is the disconnect? Why has the church eagerly taken over what parents have released? Understanding where this breakdown occurs and why it happens is the key toward building a healthy partnership in the spiritual formation of children.

Many parents feel uncomfortable about teaching their children the Bible or discussing spiritual issues. Generally, their discomfort is rooted in one of the three following areas: intimidation, lack of knowledge, or fear of not having all the right answers. People like to feel confident about what they do, and when there is a deficit of confidence, they tend to disengage or not even try. Rather than take over, the church must engage parents and give them the confidence that not only can they do it, but they must do it.

Churches can approach partnering with parents through a simple system of inspiration, equipping, and support. One of the greatest roles a children's pastor can fill is to inspire parents by giving them hope that they can make a difference in their child's life. Parents not only need to know that they should lead their kids spiritually, but they also need to know that they can be successful at it. Children's pastors can equip parents by coming alongside and guiding them through each step of spiritual development and offering advice, resources, and tools. Lastly and most importantly, the church can provide the support each and every family needs through fostering community where parents are encouraged through prayer, God's Word, and love.

INSPIRE

As children's ministers, we must give family members hope. Parents need encouragement so they, too, can investigate God's Word with their children without feeling the need to be a Bible scholar. Parents have great potential to influence their children, so they must be encouraged to let the Bible be alive and active in their lives so that they can transfer this truth in the lives of their kids.

One of the best ways to inspire a parent is to get him or her involved in a way that isn't intimidating. For example, this past year my church started a new program for upper elementary and youth who are taking our baptism class. We asked that a parent stay with his or her child during the class so he or she could be involved. The feedback from the parents has been incredible. Parents enjoy the time with their kids while learning alongside them, and many have felt their spiritual relationship with their kids has been deepened. This kind of experience, where the church provides a venue for spiritual conversations, may provide a starting place for parents to continue similar conversations at home.

My church also gives parents a chance to serve in the kids' ministry. Engaging parents to serve in the children's ministry has many incredible benefits. Serving in the church gives parents confidence in how to communicate spiritual truths to children. Over time, they become more comfortable with the Bible stories and even answering the difficult questions kids ask. This experience gained transfers directly to conversations parents can have with their own kids at home. In some cases, entire families can serve in some of the younger age groups. Not only do the spiritual truths come to life in a totally different way for a family who is teaching, but also serving binds a family together and gives them something meaningful and significant to do together. This kind of experience allows families to live out their faith together, and it relationally engages the whole family in a powerful way.

EQUIP

Not only should we inspire parents, but we must also equip parents and family members with the tools for accomplishing the final goal of a Christ-centered lifestyle. We cannot lead efficiently without help from others. We have to have an army of workers to assist us in accomplishing this goal for the families who come to our church. We need mentors for leading small groups, leaders for teaching, and leaders who can walk alongside parents. With an army of leaders like that, we can equip parents by teaching them through family-training classes, by providing family activities that nurture family development, and by giving them chances to have fun as a family.

One summer, my team and I decided to have a weekend-long, family-style vacation Bible school. This was done off campus at a local park at the beginning of the summer. The families had uninterrupted time together outside of their normal routine, which gave them time to focus on just their family through games, Bible study, and loads of activities. Because of the fun we all had, even we leaders who had set all this up wanted to start up a regular Sunday-afternoon meet-up in the park for the rest of the summer.

Another effective method for equipping parents is to establish family-training classes. Family-training classes help parents guide their children as they grow in their relationships with Jesus Christ. Training can consist of classes, seminars, and information posted on the church webpage or in an informational flyer passed out to new families. As we equip families, it's important that we take time to continually assess the needs of both individuals and families in our church community.

Families are in a constant forward motion nowadays. It's vital that we be intentional about what opportunities we provide for families to connect. Not only will our church attendance rise, but there will also be more families coming together with their kids and enjoying church. The church's goal should not be to make families feel as if they need to attend all classes and activities but to equip families with instruction on how to live a godly lifestyle in today's world.

SUPPORT

Once we have inspired and equipped the parents of our church, we need to lend parents a hand as we come alongside them through their parental journey. Here is a place we can train some of our leaders who are gifted in nurturing others to be mentors to younger parents. A mentoring program can easily be established by using older parents that have the wisdom, insight, and experience to help families. While I am fortunate to have my parents nearby, I have found that many people live a distance from their own parents and miss that support.

While I was serving in our MOPS (Mothers of Preschoolers) program, we recruited the older mothers to mentor the young mothers. This was a huge success. Each group had a leader and a mentor mom to facilitate the group. During discussions, so much good Biblical advice came from the leader and the mentor mom. Ladies who didn't live near their parents appreciated the advice, love, and support from their mentor moms. In fact, I am still in contact with my mentor mom, and I enjoy our relationship even though my mom lives close. It's a blessing to take time with my mentor for a coffee during a crazy-busy week to help me refocus on what I have been working on. I see it as God's way to gently remind me it's His work, not mine.

Although the church may have stepped over its boundaries in years past and attempted to be something it was never intended to be in the life of kids, there's no doubt that the church is the absolute best place to engage families in spiritual matters. This may mean that our children's ministries need to reshape some of our priorities. We might need to spend less time developing that new kidmin discipleship program and figure out how we can better resource parents. Our parents need to be inspired in a way they've not been before. They must see that they've got what it takes to be successful. They need great resources and tools that are simple enough to implement at home. Lastly, they need a system of support, one that the church can easily provide. When we make this our focus, we align our priorities with God's plan for the spiritual formation of children, and we give the children in our churches the best opportunities for long-term success.

Your Eric Trap

Don't fall into the same trap as Eric. Go beyond reading inspirational words and stories, and measure your life and ministry against the traps many in ministry fall into as did Eric. Open up your journal or notebook, and take time to answer the questions below. Allow the principles in this chapter to translate into the context of your life and ministry.

Evaluate your church's ministry to families. In what ways does your church intentionally empower parents to lead their kids spiritually? In what ways does your church take the spiritual leadership role away from parents?

Make a list of 3-5 resources that parents need most from the church in regard to their children and parenting. Conduct some research. Poll at least ten families inside and outside the church (with children of various ages) about what they need most from the church in regard to their children and parenting. How are your list and the list from your research similar? How are the two lists different? What is your takeaway?

What are three simple things you can implement this week that values parents in their role as spiritual leaders of the home?

What are three initiatives that can be developed over the next 12-24 months that inspire, equip, and support parents in their role as spiritual leaders of the home?

When it comes to developing an effective family ministry, what's next for you? What books do you need to read? What conference/seminar do you need to attend? What conversations do you need to have?

Wednesday

WEDNESDAY, FEBRUARY 20TH, 7:32 A.M.

Eric hit the snooze button for the fifth time. It wasn't the annoying beeping that finally woke him; it was the light streaming in from the space between the shade and his window frame. Eric lay there contemplating his week. It had been one of those weeks where an extra couple of minutes to lie in bed and think would make all the difference, so he did. Eric rolled over and glanced at his radio alarm clock, 7:32. Eric took a moment to process that time. "7:32!" he started. With eyes wide open and his heart thumping in his chest, he lunged out of bed.

Eric threw an old pair of jeans on and ran to EJ's room. His firstborn was sound asleep. *Oh, to be a teenager again*, Eric thought to himself. Eric made his way to EJ's bed avoiding land mines of clothing, books, video-game cartridges, and more. He began shaking EJ out of his slumber. "Seriously, you'd sleep through an earthquake, wouldn't you?" Eric questioned as EJ finally began stirring.

"What?"

"Nothing. Hey bud, you're late for school. Get up and hit the shower. Your dad overslept too."

"Okay, I'm up," EJ groaned as Eric stumbled out of the room, tripping over a pile of dirty laundry.

As Eric rounded the corner and headed down the stairs, Rebecca called from the kitchen, "Eric, honey, I made coffee. Is EJ up? Don't forget, his marching-band performance is in less than an hour."

Eric skidded to a halt at the bottom of the stairs, "What's that, honey?"

Rebecca kissed Eric on the cheek. "I said that I made coffee for you. I've got the girls in the car already. I'm going to drop them off at school on my way to the doctor."

"Oh yeah, I forgot. Okay, sounds good. I'll see you tonight after work."

Rebecca turned to walk out the door to the garage. "You better get a move on, sweetie. EJ's band director doesn't tolerate tardiness. Remember, his performance starts at 8:30."

Eric looked at her with a blank stare. "This morning?"

With frustration in her voice, Rebecca shot back, "Eric! Yes, I put it on your calendar. Remember? We talked about this last week. His performance is at 8:30 on Wednesday morning. I can't believe you forgot."

Eric grabbed fistfuls of hair in frustration. "Crud, I totally overlooked it; I am so sorry. I'm not sure I'm going to be able to make it, I've got to get my monthly financials turned in before noon, and I've got the kids pastors' lunch today as well. What time is your appointment at the doctor?"

Rebecca put her hands on her hips. "Excuse me? Are you trying to weasel out of your son's band performance? Eric, it took me three months to get this doctor's appointment. I can't reschedule."

Eric crossed his arms. "Rebecca, come on. It's going to take me at least two hours to get my financials turned in, and if I don't, we won't get that reimbursement check until next week. Plus, you know I have to lead the kids pastors' lunch today, so I've got to be there a little early. Can't you cancel?"

Rebecca snatched her keys with one hand and put her hand on the door to the garage with the other. "Eric, I'm not going to cancel my appointment. We talked about this before. I can't hold your hand through your inability to follow your own calendar. You're a big boy. Figure it out!" With that, she walked out into the garage pulling the door forcibly behind her.

"Great, I will!" Eric shouted loud enough for her to hear him.

Eric walked toward the stairs and called up to his son "EJ, I don't hear the shower. Grab your clothes and get washed up. We need to leave in ten minutes."

"Dad, I need my band uniform. Can you get it for me?" EJ asked.

"Where is it?"

"I don't know. The laundry room?"

Eric headed to the laundry room and began rummaging through piles of clean unfolded laundry. He couldn't help but think, *What does she do all day?* He quickly pushed aside his frustration and focused on finding EJ's uniform. After what seemed like hours, he finally found it. Wrinkled.

"When it rains it pours," he muttered.

He yanked the ironing board down and plugged in the iron. "EJ," he yelled, "I'm ironing it now. You better be ready to go when I'm finished." Eric began haphazardly running the iron over the biggest wrinkles.

Two short minutes later, EJ called downstairs, "Dad, you almost done?" Eric pushed the iron over the last wrinkled sleeve. "Come on, I'm going to be late!"

Eric snapped the iron cord from the wall and raced upstairs. It was 8:05. He tossed the uniform to EJ, "Done. Put this thing on, and I'll meet you in the car. I'll grab the OJ and a banana. No time for eggs."

Depending on traffic, it usually only took six to ten minutes to get to Jim Irwin Middle School. This morning Eric knew it was going to be close, really close. Mr. Jacobs, EJ's band director, was known for requiring tardy students to play scales the entire duration of class. One time, when four or five students came in late, he required the entire class to play scales as punishment. Eric didn't want EJ to get into trouble, so he knew he'd have to drive as fast as he could.

The ride to school was very quiet. EJ's eyes kept darting to the dashboard clock while he drummed his hands on the door handle. They pulled into the drop-off lane at 8:14. "Yes!" EJ exclaimed, "I'm gonna make it."

"Thanks a million, Dad! The last thing I want on performance day is to be late. No telling what Mr Jacobs would've done."

"No problem, EJ. That's what dad's do, right?"

EJ smiled. "Dad, you can park along 9th Street for the performance. It's less of a walk than the visitor lot."

Eric frowned. "EJ, I'm not sure I'm going to be able to make it. I've got some deadlines this morning and a really important meeting at lunch that I have to get ready for."

EJ's smile evaporated.

"EJ, I know. Dad totally messed up with this one."

"Mom said you were going to come."

"I know, Son. I'm sorry. I'll make the next one. I promise."

Tears started to well up in EJ's eyes. He quickly turned his face away from Eric and said, "Okay, sure, Dad. Well, I've gotta go. I'm gonna be late." He grabbed his backpack from the backseat and ran toward the building.

"Good luck, EJ!" Eric shouted as his son disappeared.

"Guess I'm not going to win the father-of-the-year trophy this year," Eric said to himself as he put the car into gear. Although he tried to shrug it off, he felt like a jerk—a big, fat jerk.

On his drive into the office, Eric's thoughts focused on his family. It had been a rough couple of months. Church had been extra busy, and he'd been working a lot of late hours. The load was suffocating, and his family was definitely feeling the effects.

As he pulled into the church parking lot, his thoughts turned to his day. The weekend was coming up, so he had lots of stuff to fix before Sunday. Plus, he had to finish that paperwork, and before he knew it, it was going to be time for the kids pastors' lunch. Eric had been instrumental in getting this Houston Metro Kids Pastors' Network going a couple of years ago. He was proud of his little group that had grown from four to sixteen.

Eric shifted the car into park. He took a deep breath. It has been a rough week so far, but it was Wednesday, and he was confident things were going to turn around. They had to.

He walked into the church building. As he headed to his office, Florence greeted him with a smile, his mail, and a cup of coffee. Florence really was amazing. Not that anyone had asked or expected her to do this, but she always took care of the staff in her own unique ways. For Eric, most days she greeted him at his office with a hot cup of coffee and his mail.

Eric smiled back and asked Florence how she was doing. After a short round of pleasantries, he asked Florence if she could hold his calls. Time was ticking away, and he had some deadlines to hit before he had to leave for lunch.

Eric put his check requests and budget summaries in the finance box a little ahead of schedule, which was perfect because it gave him extra time to prepare for the network meeting. Eric sat at his desk thinking through all that had happened that week. From Jim's temper tantrum in the hall to missing EJ's performance, Eric felt a twinge of isolation. Volunteers were quitting; his pastor was taking sides against him when he needed his support most; and the stress of work was taking its toll on his home life. As much as he tried, Eric could not keep his thoughts from drifting to his calling. Eric always felt he was called to be a children's pastor, but weeks like this one made him wonder, *Did I miss something?*

Eric spent the next fifteen minutes in prayer and meditation.

11:35 A.M. THE NETWORK LUNCH

Eric got into his car at eleven and started toward the Waffle House. What could he say? He had a soft spot in his heart for Waffle House. From fond memories of cramming during Bible college to staying up late to discuss the finer points of theology with a few close friends, the Waffle House was like a second home. It was those fond memories, not the menu, which prompted Eric to start the kids pastors' network lunch there in the first place. It probably wasn't the best place for a network lunch, but as long as Eric was leading the charge, that's where they'd meet.

Eric got there a few minutes before everyone else. He sat in the car and began calling the latest graduating class of New Hope's membership class. He was leaking volunteers like a poorly constructed diaper, and he needed some fresh faces. He figured contacting new members was the best place to start.

Over the next few minutes, his table filled up with local kids' pastors. There were lots of handshakes, hugs, and small talk. The small talk consisted mostly of what everyone did with their spouses for Valentine's Day and how the Texan's let the Super Bowl slip though their hands. Slowly, everyone found a seat, and, finally, everyone placed his or her order.

As they waited for their food, the conversation turned toward work. People discussed attendance dips, budget cuts, summer programs, and everything else in between. Eric didn't want to get into a my-week-was-worse-than-yours duel with the pastor next to him, so he decided to go ahead and kick off the meeting.

He cleared his throat. "While we are waiting for our food, I thought we could talk about how things are going in our churches. I've had one of those you-can't-tweet-this-but-if-you-could-people-would-retweet-it kind of weeks. Seriously, off the record, my week started when one of my best workers blew a gasket in the middle of the hall in front of kids, parents, and other team members. The crazy part is that I was considering this guy for a staff position. He has all the talent in the world, but he has a severe lack of judgment and people skills."

Sally, a forty-something children's pastor who just passed the five-year mark asked, "What did you do?"

"I just minimized the damage and did my best to preserve the little dignity that he had left. I'm not going to lie. It was a mess," Eric responded. "I guess I'm just grateful I found out how much of a hothead he was before I put him on staff."

"Sounds intense," Sally said.

"That's not even the worse part. My preschool director decided to quit the very next day. She had been thinking about it, and the episode in the hall pushed her over the edge. She sent me her resignation via e-mail."

Several shook their heads in disbelief.

"Luckily, my negotiation skills paid off, and I talked her into staying. You know what else? My pastor thinks that this hothead volunteer is right. Although he didn't come right out and say it, he pretty much insinuated that this was all my fault. Can you believe that?"

Dave, a recent seminary grad and kids' pastor for less then a year chimed in, "Your pastor really said that?"

"Yeah, pretty much. He encouraged me to pray about how I can do things differently so it doesn't happen again. The crazy part is that I've worked my tail off for this church for *years*. I met with a family for lunch yesterday, and they were singing my praises, but my own pastor thinks I'm to blame. I'm not out looking for pats on the back, but this isn't the kind of recognition anyone deserves." Something inside Eric told him to stop, but sharing with a group of colleagues all the stuff he'd been through that week was cathartic.

Eric surprised himself when he heard his voice catch while saying, "I have done nothing but give everything I have to this church. I personally fought for and oversaw the renovation of our children's wing. I went before the board and got them to see the benefit of our new computerized check-in. And what do I get for it? A crazy volunteer blows up on me, and my pastor thinks I should apologize to him. Am I nuts for thinking like this?"

It was quiet for a few moments. Fellow children's pastors looked at Eric with concern. Mike, who was sitting right beside Eric, put his arm around his shoulder.

Bill, the senior member of the group filled the awkward silence. "Eric, I think that all of us have been in similar situations. It's never easy when you feel like you are doing everything, yet no one else sees. It's tough to put your heart into every weekend, and there is never a mention of how you're doing until there is a problem." Eric nodded in agreement. He could feel his eyes welling up.

Bill spoke with such warmth and compassion. Out of all the other pastors in their networking group, Eric respected Bill most. Bill had been a successful kids' pastor on every level. He had worked in a local church and saw God do great things. He had also spoken at many different conferences, and even though he was one of the more senior guys in the group, he was very tech savvy with his iPhone™, and recently he had been mentoring other kids' pastors through his blog. The fact that he was older and still valued technology impressed Eric.

Bill continued, "Eric, one of the reasons I come to this gathering you started is for this very reason; we all need each other at different times. You clearly need us right now. Why don't we gather around Eric and pray for him." Everyone got up and circled around Eric and took turns praying and encouraging their fellow brother. Bill finished praying with an authoritative, "Amen!"

As everyone found their seats, the food was delivered to their table, and they began eating and talking amongst themselves.

Once lunch was finished, most made their way over to Eric and shook his hand or gave him an encouraging hug before they left. When only a few people were left, Eric asked Bill if he had a couple of minutes to talk. Eric wanted to ask him some important questions.

Bill ordered another refill while Eric returned to the table after seeing the rest of his ministry pals off. He settled in the booth with Bill, and an awkward silence followed. Eric didn't know where to start, so he was relieved when Bill broke the silence and asked him what was on his mind.

"Well," Eric began, "as you could probably could tell from today, I am beyond frustrated with my situation. I feel like I am the only one who values kids' ministry in my church. I thought that at least my pastor believed in what I was doing, but with him taking the side of my volunteer over me, it makes me wonder why he didn't give me the benefit of the doubt instead."

Eric paused to make sure what he was saying made sense, but Bill didn't ask any questions, he just said, "Go on."

Eric continued, "I have built our kids' ministry from just a handful of kids to a program that many people respect and, I suspect, some even envy. I would really like to find out from you how you started speaking at conferences, writing books, and even blog. I know that a lot of people read your blog, and I have been thinking about doing something like that for a long time. After a week like this, I feel that I need to start pursuing this stuff. You know, working toward whatever is next. You seem to have a lot of influence in your church and around the country. How do you do it? What steps did you take to get where you are now?"

Bill was quiet.

Eric finally asked, "So do you have any advice for me?"

Bill took a deep breath and said, "Eric, let me start by saying I think you are one of the most gifted kids' pastors I have ever met. You have much more raw, God-given talent at your age than I ever had when I was a young buck."

Eric smiled, somewhat embarrassed by the compliment but also wondering what was coming on the other side.

Bill continued, "There are a few things, however, I think you need to know in order to be successful on a national level."

Eric was ready; this was the stuff he had been waiting for.

"Eric, you're having a rough week. I get that, and I've been there. Because of this week, or season, you're beginning to look for an exit plan. Mark my words, Eric Newman, you need to push through this and come out on the other side."

Eric stared blankly at Bill. "What are you saying?"

Bill smiled and said, "Eric, you need to serve your pastor. That is your first priority at New Hope."

Eric felt like someone punched him in the gut. Was Bill even paying attention when Eric described how his pastor had betrayed him?

"Are you familiar with the old saying that all politics are local?"

Eric shot back, "Yeah, but what does that have to do with anything?"

"Well, Eric, one of the reasons I believe God has blessed me with all the opportunities you mentioned earlier is I believe that all ministry is local. I believe the local church is the hope of the world. It's my job to support my pastor and build a local church that Jesus would be proud of. If I can do that part well, everything else will come in due time."

"Of course. I get it. That's why I got into kids' ministry in the first place."

Bill jumped in, "I'm not sure you do get it."

Eric tried to mask a puzzled and frustrated look on his face.

"I'm not judging you here. I don't know your entire situation, but a kids' pastor who is serving his or her pastor doesn't say the kinds of things you said today in front of this group. A children's pastor who is serving his pastor may struggle privately, but he or she praises publicly."

Eric lowered his head. He felt the sting of truth. Although he didn't agree with Pastor Wheeler on some points, he did enjoy working for him. He immediately began to regret some of the things he had said.

Bill continued, "I'm not going to say anything more about that. I think you get the point I was trying to make. However, I feel I need to say something else.

"I've made another observation. I hear your desire to do something beyond New Hope. That's admirable, and there's nothing wrong in general with wanting to serve the church. However, before you gain a voice beyond our little community, there's something you need to know."

Eric wasn't sure what to expect. Although this conversation with Bill wasn't going in the direction he had planned, he was pretty sure this was stuff he needed to know.

Bill went on, "I heard everything you said today, and I think you have a measurement problem. I think you are measuring your success based on all the wrong things. I also think that if you don't learn how to measure the right things, anything you say in a book or a blog will do more harm than good.

"I heard you talk a lot about how many kids are coming, your computerized check-in, your new kids' wing, and how good of a communicator you are. Those things are great assets to have under your belt; however, we can't measure our success by those things alone."

Eric replied, "I don't get it. I assumed that those things were measures of success. If I were to put together my resume, those would be some of the things I'd put down." Annoyed, Eric continued. "If we don't measure by those things, how are we supposed to know if we are being effective? I have, on more than one occasion, heard you talk about how many kids your kids' ministry grew by."

"Easy, Eric, I am not trying to accuse you of anything. I am just trying to tell you what I hope someone would tell me if I were in your place. What we measure with makes all the difference."

Bill paused for a minute. "Like I was saying earlier, those things you mentioned are not bad in and of themselves, but most of them are simply tools or indicators. It doesn't really take that much to remodel a building, buy fancy new equipment, or gather a big crowd. Those things aren't bad, but they're not what is most important."

"Let me break it down this way. In all my years of doing children's ministry, I have learned a couple of things I try to never forget. Even more importantly, I try to pass them along to others like I'm doing for you right now. First of all, always support your pastor. If you find yourself in a place where you no longer do, it's time that you find another pastor who you can support. Second, our effectiveness is not measured by the tools we use but by life change that results from the tools we may or may not have. Third, life change is not measured in weeks and months but rather in years and decades. And finally, your family is the best indication of your success in life and ministry."

Eric felt numb. Although it was only four simple statements, it was a lot to process. "Wow, no one has ever shared anything like that with me before. You should write a book about these things."

Bill smiled, "I am."

"Ha!" Eric exclaimed. "Well, let me know when you are done. I'll buy the first copy."

Bill leaned in on his elbows, "Eric, I know this may be a lot right now, but if you commit yourself to these things, I am confident that you will be a success no matter who takes notice."

As he was speaking, Eric's phone chimed reminding him he had a 1:30 appointment at the church. "Bill, thank you so much for your time. You certainly have given me a lot to think about. Could you do me a favor?"

"Sure, name it."

"Could you email me those four things?"

"Absolutely."

"Well, I've gotta go. Duty calls. See you next month, and I'll be looking forward to that e-mail."

Eric paid his bill and then jumped in his car. His head was spinning. He replayed all the conversations from the previous week through the filter of what he'd just learned from Bill. It was disappointing for sure. Maybe Bill was right. Maybe he wasn't. Maybe it was just Bill's experience. Grace Point, where Bill had served for all those years, was a very different church from New Hope. Maybe all of this stuff didn't really apply, at least not entirely. Were the four things Bill shared words of wisdom that worked for a different generation? Ministry was moving a lot faster than it was twenty years ago. How timeless could his wisdom be?

Eric felt pretty beat up in spite of having poured every ounce of his heart into ministry. He was having a difficult time determining how much of what Bill said could really make a difference in his situation. The part about measurement was especially intriguing. He couldn't shake the idea of life change being measured in the context of years and decades as opposed to weeks and days. Eric knew he had to spend some time contemplating the complexity of that statement. At the very least, it would make a good tweet.

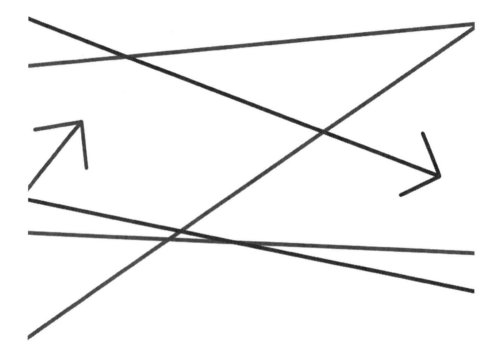

Chapter 4: Measuring Success

KRISTIN ENGLUND

We are a culture that loves numbers. All around us we can see examples of how we are obsessed with wins and losses, GPAs and SAT scores, stock market values, Facebook™ friends, and pounds and inches. In many ways, we measure success by numbers. Numbers can set you apart from the person next to you and set your church apart from the one down the street. Numbers have the ability to make or break us.

As someone who has always struggled with my weight, I know all about the number game. As early as elementary school, I was aware that I was overweight, and I wanted to change that. I cared about numbers and wanted to reach my goals. Numbers can be good; in weight loss, numbers certainly are indicators of success. Dropping 15, 25, or 50 pounds can make a big difference. However, the number is not the real goal. If you're all about the number, then you're missing the point. In the world of weight loss, the point is to get healthy. That is the real reason for the early mornings at the gym, the smaller portions at dinner, and saying no to that piece of cake (or at least that second piece of cake). Getting healthy is the motivation, the reason to care about the numbers.

What we measure makes all the difference. In ministry, it is easy to get caught up in the numbers. It's easy to define success by the size of our children's church or the dollars in our budget line. Success may be a computerized check-in system, a themed children's wing, or the biggest fall festival in town. When meeting someone from another church, we often get the vitals first. We ask how many kids are in their ministry, one campus or two, which curriculum they use, and how many staff members they have. The list goes on.

While each one of these numbers is good and can be an indicator of a vibrant ministry, numbers alone cannot be the goal. If we only go after the numbers, we miss the point. We need to align our thinking to God's definition of success and continue to set our hearts right before Him as we plan and lead.

Think back to when you first sensed a call to serve the Lord in the local church. Where did you find your excitement, and where did you sense God working through you most? Maybe it was in front of a room full of kids sharing about Christ's sacrifice on the cross. Maybe it was praying with a child whose parents had just divorced. Maybe it was meeting with some parents who were overwhelmed with the responsibilities looming just ahead with the birth of their first child. For you, which moments stand out?

More than likely, we all entered into ministry because we wanted to see lives changed. We wanted to see children come to know Christ and follow Him for their whole lives. We wanted to be part of God's work to heal hurting families and turn hearts back to Him. Life change is what ministry is all about. The tools that we use are just that, tools. They help accomplish the great work God desires to do in the people of our churches and of our communities. Whether it's the newest technology, the most impressive ministry environment, or the top-of-the-line curriculum, the tools are not the end goal.

Our chief goal, our ultimate end, is to serve the Lord Jesus Christ with everything we have. We are to love Him and love people. Success in ministry is not the numbers that come through our doors or the tools that we use; it is lives that are changed. It is the children that come to know the living God, the families that are transformed, and the hearts that are set on fire for the gospel.

We need to measure success in our ministry in light of this goal. Every decision we make and every dream we pursue needs to be done with a clear purpose to serve Christ and see lives changed. No matter where our ministry is today, whether we have 15 kids, 150, or 1,500, we have the same challenge.

Should we measure numbers? Absolutely. Should we go after new tools to enhance our ministries? Most definitely. We should use everything available to us, all of the creativity we can muster, to teach the gospel in new ways and to reach families from the community who are un-churched. Being aware of numbers can help us see trends and understand the effectiveness of our ministries. We should track and evaluate to help us get a picture of what God is doing in our churches.

As we evaluate our numbers, we need to be very careful to not allow pride to creep in, something that can be incredibly easy to fall victim to. In fact, it's something I'm far too familiar with. This past year in my church we saw a 13 percent growth in regularly attending children and families. Everyone was excited about this number, and it motivated and encouraged us to continue to improve and strengthen our programs to effectively minister among the increase in kids. Seeing growth and being part of it forced me to battle with pride each day. I had to come before God and turn my definition of success and my view of numbers to Him.

This is something each one of us in ministry must be intentional about. We need to check ourselves to make sure we understand success correctly. It's really a heart issue. We need to get right these three essentials in order to align our hearts with God's definition of success.

1. WE NEED TO THRIVE SPIRITUALLY.

One of the main ways that we can lose sight of true success in ministry is by getting off track with God. When we serve God in the local church, it's easy to think that every day spent in the office or every day teaching will automatically make us grow closer to God. I've found that this just isn't true.

Just because we work in a church or volunteer our time doesn't mean we get a free pass when it comes to spiritual growth. It is vital for us as leaders in ministry to have an active, personal spiritual life. My favorite picture of this is in John 15. Jesus describes our relationship with Him like a vine and branches. Jesus calls us to abide in Him, to cling to Him. I love how The Message describes Jesus' words in verse four, "Live in me. Make your home in me just as I do in you." We, as ministers, need to cling tightly to the vine, to Christ. Each day we need to rely fully on Christ to do the work He has called us to do.

For me, this is something I have to be very intentional about because I learned the hard way I couldn't do it alone. It was just before Vacation Bible School two years ago that I reached a low point in my ministry. My schedule was overwhelming, and the task list ahead of me was daunting. I had lost the sense of joy I usually had when leading; instead everything felt like a chore. Things that before came easily to me felt like an uphill battle. I realized that for several weeks I had really let my time with God slip. In the busyness of ministry, I had stopped spending intentional time with God. I wasn't abiding in Him. The result was that I was leading totally on my own strength. The task ahead of me was great, and I felt the enormity of it. Thankfully, God was faithful to bring me back into closeness with Him. I felt the heavy burden of ministry lift, and, once again I experienced joy as I served Him.

The greatest error we can make is to begin leading in our own strength. We will not succeed if we plan and lead unless we are closely connected to Christ. The key to success is to pursue intimacy with Christ before anything else and to allow our entire ministry to flow out of that relationship.

2. WE NEED TO CARE FOR THE FLOCK GOD HAS GIVEN US.

It can be very easy to get caught up in the paperwork, planning, and execution of ministry in the church. Children's ministry certainly has a wealth of to-dos and tasks that can fill up our schedules. There are always copies to be made, craft materials to be purchased, events to be planned, and volunteers to be recruited. If we spend most of our time in the office getting things ready for the coming weeks, it can be easy to lose sight of those God has called us to serve. As ministers, we are called to shepherd the flock that God has placed in our care. (1 Peter 5:2.) One of our primary responsibilities is to care for and lead the people God has given us.

The flock God has given you depends on your role in your church. It may be your staff team, your volunteer leaders, or the small group of kids you teach. In order to care for this flock, you first need to identify who they are. Take a minute to write down those who directly report to you in your ministry environment. It may be helpful to map out your team structure. Who are the people that you formally look out for? These are people that should be high on your priority list.

What does it mean to shepherd the flock God has given to us? We need to be intentional to pray for and build relationships with the people God has given to us. If someone is in need, we should care for him or her as Christ would. We might need to put down our to-do lists, set some paperwork aside, and take one of our volunteers out for coffee. Maybe we need to fill in as a small-group leader to connect with some of the kids in our ministries. Whatever we do, we must be intentional about caring for the flock God has given us. At the end of the day, we won't ever regret making that phone call, writing that sympathy card, or praying with that child.

Caring for the flock God has given us is essential to align our hearts to God's definition of success. If success is measured in life change, we need to be part of changing lives.

3. WE NEED TO SUBMIT OUR DREAMS AND PLANS TO GOD.

Close your eyes and imagine your ministry five years from now. What do you see? Maybe you see double the number of kids rushing through the doors. Maybe you see three new campuses across your city. Maybe you see a vibrant parent ministry. Maybe you see your church as a central location in your city where those in need know they can find help. What is it that you see? Are you willing to ask God what He wants to do through you, your staff, and your volunteers in the coming years?

As leaders, God desires to use us to accomplish His purposes. We may have dreams that are bigger than what we can imagine possible. As we think about the dreams that we have for our lives and our ministries, it is vital that we submit those dreams to His authority. God has a plan for each one of our lives, and He desires to use us to make a difference in His kingdom.

Maybe you've never given Him the opportunity to show you what dreams He has for your life. If that's the case, come before God and ask Him to give you a vision for ministry that is bigger than you are.

Knowing God desires to use us, we want to be sure to follow after these dreams and live them out in complete submission to Him. A key to measuring success in ministry by God's definition is to submit each decision we make to His authority. The plans that we make should all be brought before Him before we act. We should be careful to do nothing with planning or goal setting until we have submitted it to the Lord. If we make this a priority, then our ministry decisions will be in line with His definition of success.

God is in the business of changing lives and drawing people into relationship with Him. As ministers in the local church, we have the exciting opportunity to be part of that. Measuring success in ministry is about life change, not just numbers for the sake of numbers, or tools for the sake of tools. It can be easy for us to lose our focus on Christ and begin to operate in our own strength. We can, at times, forget our call as shepherds of God's flock and fail to care for those He has given us. We can put limits on God's dreams for us or fail to submit our plans to Him. In ministry, it's easy to fall into the trap of being all about the numbers. We can allow the numbers to define success; but if we do that, we miss the point.

Falling into this trap does not mean we fall out of the faithful hands of our loving Father. Wherever we are today and in whatever ministry situation we are serving, we know that our steps are ordered by the Lord. God has called us where we are today for a purpose, and He desires for us to be faithful with what He has asked of us. If we will abide in Him and give Him our plans, He will guide us as we lead our ministry by His definition of success.

Your Eric Trap

Don't fall into the same trap as Eric. Go beyond reading inspirational words and stories, and measure your life and ministry against the traps many in ministry fall into as did Eric. Open up your journal or notebook, and take time to answer the questions below. Allow the principles in this chapter to translate into the context of your life and ministry.

What has been your definition of success in ministry? How does this align with God's definition of success? Where do these two definitions vary? What steps do you need to take to align your definition of success with God's definition of success?

What is your personal spiritual temperature? Are you moving closer to God or further away?

Who are you directly responsible for spiritually? How have you lead these people spiritually? What three things can you do/change to maximize your impact on their lives?

List three to five dreams you have for yourself or your ministry for the next twelve to twenty-four months. Commit each dream to prayer this week (or for several weeks). What does it seem like the Lord is saying in regard to each one?

List three to five dreams you have for yourself or your ministry for the next five to ten years. Commit each dream to prayer this week (or for several weeks). What does it seem like the Lord saying in regard to each one?

Thursday

THURSDAY, FEBRUARY 21ST, 10:13 A.M.

Eric stared blankly out the window overlooking Rawlings Park. It was a dreary winter morning. He was in his favorite seat at his favorite coffee shop. The entire west wall of the coffee shop was a glass overlook of a beautiful neighborhood park. Eric liked to sit at the bar, which afforded him both a great view and a wall outlet for his laptop. This time, however, his laptop was in the car.

The cold drizzle combined with the gray morning reflected his mood, somber with a twinge of hopelessness. It had been a rough week for sure, but there had been some good moments scattered about. Unfortunately, things had taken a turn for the worse the day before. At 4:00, he had gotten a text from Rebecca.

> *I cant express how mad i am right now. EJ told me u didn't come 2 his performance. Seriously? U blew off your own son? Who are u?*

Eric had just stared at the text. In that moment, so many emotions had flooded through his head. He'd felt like a complete and total jerk. He'd let his son down. He'd let Rebecca down. He was overwhelmed with disappointment, and the pit in his stomach had made him wish he could go back and do the day over.

Oppressed by guilt, other thoughts had begun to cloud his mind. He reasoned that Rebecca had painted him into a corner. She knew his schedule was full of things that could not have been changed; changing her appointment would have been the easiest. Why had she been so stubborn about not changing her appointment? But then he remembered that a no-show at the doctor would have cost them another hundred dollars, and it wouldn't have been the first time Eric or Rebecca had canceled at the last minute. Actually, every cancellation had always been because of Eric's busy schedule, more specifically, Eric's failure to communicate his schedule with Rebecca, which had been a hot topic for years.

As much as Eric would have liked an excuse or way out, there was no denying it. Eric had been to blame. He had been the jerk. Rebecca was furious, and EJ was hurt. That was EJ's third performance of the year, and Eric hadn't made it to any.

Eric had texted his wife back:

> *Who am I? Wow, that hurts! Im sorry! I really am. Please, can we talk about it tonight?*

Eric had waited for a reply, but nothing came. Just before 6:00, he had packed up his things and headed home. He'd texted Rebecca two more times and called once. She didn't answer. Eric knew that he was in trouble. He and Rebecca had a great relationship, but like most couples, they had had some rough patches; this was clearly another rough patch.

This had even happened before. About three years back, Eric had forgotten their anniversary, and Rebecca just disappeared for half of the day. She didn't return phone calls or texts. She just took her time and gathered her thoughts. When she was ready, she had let him have it. Eric knew that was coming again.

When Eric had arrived at home, the house was dark. Rebecca and the kids hadn't arrived home. Eric had thought about calling Rebecca's sister or mom, both of whom lived in town. More than likely, his family was at one of their houses. But what if they weren't? What if he called Rebecca's sister and they weren't with her? Then she'd be concerned, and she'd start calling and texting Rebecca who would probably get through only to hear about the class-A jerk Eric had been.

Rebecca's mother would have been even worse. Eric had just decided to wait it out.

At 7:45, the minivan had pulled into the driveway. The door opened, and out poured the Newman family. Eric wasn't sure what to expect, so he had remained seated at the kitchen table dispensing hugs and high fives to the kids as they came through the kitchen door. EJ just rolled his eyes, dropped his backpack by the door, and ran up the stairs to his bedroom. Eric knew he deserved that.

Finally Rebecca entered. Eric had braced himself as best he could without giving himself away, but what happened next, he hadn't expected. Rebecca walked into the kitchen with her jaw set and went right past Eric without acknowledging him. She called up the stairs, "Hey kids, baths. Pajamas. Get ready for bed. Your father's in charge." Without missing a beat, she rounded the corner and headed straight to the bedroom. The door softly closed and then clicked shut. It was locked. Eric hadn't been able to move. What had just happened? Although he had been relieved that the outpouring of accusations and disappointments didn't come, he had actually felt worse because he didn't know what was going to happen and when it was going to happen.

But Eric had embraced his defeat. He got all the kids bathed and fixed himself a sandwich to eat alone in the dark kitchen. Twice he had stood outside the bedroom door for a few minutes, just wanting to go in and get it over with. Once he had heard sobbing, the kind that comes from deep in the gut. Eric had felt like a piece of trash. He'd caused that pain. Although he could be an idiot at times, he knew better than disturbing Rebecca before she was ready. Eric had finally given up when he turned in early in the guest bedroom.

Although he had been physically and emotionally exhausted, he hadn't been able to fall asleep. In his mind, he kept wrestling over the situation. Everyone was always telling him about this elusive thing called balance. But Eric couldn't think of many people who had it, and he couldn't imagine it was a remote possibility in this situation. Bill's words had echoed in his head, "Your family is the best indication of your success in life and ministry." Everything about that statement sounded right. Eric felt that it was what he wanted, but it seemed as distant as the end of a rainbow. He didn't know how to get to where he could experience that kind of success. Overall, it had been a pretty rotten week, but the pain and frustration he had felt that night, sleeping alone in the guest bedroom, was his rock bottom.

Eric took another sip of his coffee. Over and over he relived the previous day. Rebecca had been very frustrated with his schedule for months, but if he had been able to attend EJ's performance, would that have been enough, or would it have only delayed the disaster that unfolded the day before? More than anything, he wanted it all to be a distant memory.

That morning hadn't been any better. Eventually, Eric had fallen asleep sometime after 3:00 A.M. Five hours of staring at the guest-bedroom wallpaper just hadn't been dull enough to send him to sleep. Jolted awake at 7:42 to the sound of the garage door closing, he had looked out the window just in time to see Rebecca driving off to take the kids to school.

Rebecca hadn't woken him up. Eric debated what that meant: was she still so angry that she just didn't want to have to deal with him that morning, or had she been even angrier now because he hadn't left the guest bedroom to initiate a conversation or at least say goodbye to the kids before school?

Eric had sent a message to Florence telling her that he'd be coming in late. He had quickly gotten himself ready and decided to get some coffee and put some thought into what needed to happen next. This couldn't go on much longer.

More than anything, Eric wanted to have a healthy relationship with his family, and if he was being perfectly honest with himself, he knew the Newman family was anything but relationally healthy. He was at a loss as to what he could do to make things right. He could quit his job at New Hope and try to get a new job in advertising. The stress of finding a new job would be tough, but once he was working again, he'd have all the family time back.

However, Eric knew this wasn't the answer. As clearly as he knew he was supposed to marry Rebecca, he knew he was called to ministry. He knew he couldn't walk away from ministry any more than he could continue to neglect his family the way he had been. He felt stuck. He considered moving to another church. Perhaps the workload wouldn't be so overwhelming somewhere else. The thought of having his own ministry was really desirable. He thought of how great it would be to work from home while writing articles and books and developing talks for seminars and conferences. Despite Bill's advice contradicting some of Eric's thoughts and expectations, he really wished he were in a place where he could just resign and do his own thing. That would certainly help things on the family front.

At that moment, Eric's phone vibrated with an incoming text. It was Rebecca.

Come home now.

Eric felt like he was going to be sick. The wait was over. A small burden had lifted. The confrontation he had been waiting for was about to begin.

The drive home went too quickly despite his diligent adherence to the speed limits. As much as he wanted to rehearse what he was going to say, he couldn't come up with adequate words to communicate the depth of his regret. His mind was eerily silent. Was it the calm before the storm?

Eric pulled into the driveway and walked to the front door. As he put his hand on the door handle, a rush of insecurities buffeted his thoughts. *This is just a rough patch, right? We're going to be fine, I think. There hasn't been any indication that there's more to this than I expect. We both committed to a lifetime together; she still holds to that promise, right?* Eric's knees felt weak. He took a deep breath and entered.

Rebecca was sitting on the couch. To Eric's relief, she looked surprisingly calm. Void of any telling emotion, she said, "Sit down." Eric took a seat next to her on the couch.

"Eric," Rebecca began, "I think it's past time we have a very serious conversation. I'm very angry about what happened yesterday, and we'll get to that in a minute, but I feel that what is happening to our family is much bigger than your actions yesterday."

Eric quickly replied, "I know, and I'm sor—"

Rebecca help up her hand. "I'm not done. I need you to hear me before you say anything."

Eric nodded.

"It's pretty obvious that our family has been less than ideal since summer. Once school started, you've gotten busier and busier. Every time I've asked you if things were going to let up, you've said that they would in just a few weeks. Quite frankly, I'm not sure I can trust you anymore. I don't think you're intentionally being dishonest with me, but I think you're fooling yourself. This school year is over halfway through, and I feel like you've missed it. You haven't been to any of EJ's performances. None. I'm not even going to bring up Chloe's parent-teacher conference you forgot to come to. Oh, and here's something you probably don't even realize. Two weeks ago, I picked up where you left off reading *The Lion, the Witch and the Wardrobe* with Emily. You've read that book with all the kids, but after starting it with Emily in September, you hadn't even gotten past chapter three. I finally got tired of giving her excuses, so I started reading it to her."

Rebecca paused. Holding back tears, she continued, "You can ignore me and neglect me, and I'll find a way to deal with it. But when you do it to our kids, you've gone too far. If you'd only seen the look on EJ's face when I picked him up from school. You hurt him. Do you realize how out-of-control you are?"

She reached out and grabbed Eric's hand. "I'm going to be very blunt with you, Eric. You are losing us. I stand by the promise I made to you fourteen years ago, but I'm not going to let you abandon us without a fight. I need you, and, for goodness sake, the kids need you."

Eric quickly interrupted, "*Abandoned*? Don't you think that word is a little strong? I would never abandon my family."

"I don't care what it sounds like or how you want to define the word, but the truth is the truth. For the past six months, you have been here less and less, and when you are here, your mind is usually somewhere else. You may live in this house, but it's been a long time since you've really been here. I'm tired of making excuses to the kids as to why you're not at a game, performance, or bedtime duty. I feel like you've already left us."

Eric hung his head and stared at his shoes. As painful as the words were to hear, he owned them. For lack of a better word, his ministry at New Hope had become his mistress. The excitement of ministry and the burden of serving the families of his church had distracted him from his first priority, his relationship to his family.

With tears streaming down his face, he looked Rebecca in the eyes. "You're right, honey. I'm so incredibly sorry. You have been seeking me out for weeks and months, and I've not taken our situation seriously. I've not treated you or the kids fairly. I was wrong. Honey, please know that this was never my intention. I love you. I love our family, and I can't imagine a life worse than a life without you."

Rebecca gave Eric a slight smile, a ray of hope. She slid closer to him and wiped a tear away from his face with her thumb. "Thank you. I'm truly touched by your words." She paused for a few seconds. "But I really don't want your apology. More than anything, I need to know how things are going to be different."

"I know. I know. I've been thinking about this a lot lately. I really feel stuck right now. The workload I am under is intense, and, to some degree, I only feel that it's going to become more so, not less. I recognize that you and the kids have to be my first priority, not New Hope. Running at the frantic pace that I've been going at the last six months isn't an option anymore, but if I don't keep up the pace, I'll fall behind at church. I've considered going back to advertising, but I really believe that God called me into ministry, and to walk away from that isn't the right choice either."

Rebecca shook her head, "I agree. I'm not at all suggesting you walk away from ministry. God opened a lot of doors for you to do what you do, and you're a gifted children's pastor."

Eric smiled at her words. "So as I've been processing where I'm at, I'm just wondering if maybe my time is coming to an end at New Hope. In my heart, I wish I could operate my own ministry where I could work out of the house and have more time with family. I'd probably travel some, speak at conferences and do some consulting, but I know I'm still a few more years away from that. Maybe right now is the time to put my resume together again and see what opportunities are out there. I've had a great run at New Hope; possibly, I can find a church that really prioritizes the children's ministry without working its staff to death."

Rebecca said nothing. She just shook her head.

Eric leaned back a little trying to take in the signal she was sending. "What? Don't you agree?"

"No, I don't think I do," Rebecca shot back quickly but gently. "Listen, I don't think your dream of one day having your own ministry is a bad idea at all. If you feel that this is what God is leading you toward, then that's great. But obviously right now is not the time. However, I'm not completely convinced that the lack of family time is just New Hope's fault."

Eric had a stunned and confused look on his face. "Wait a second. I want to make sure I'm hearing you correctly. Are you saying that this is all my fault? Honey, I know that I've allowed my workload to overwhelm me, and I've made decisions that put you and the kids second to my work, but are you insinuating that me being worked to death is somehow my fault?"

Rebecca let out a long sigh. "No, not exactly. Well, maybe. I don't know. Please, honey, don't take this the wrong way. I've gone to the conferences with you, and I've talked to the spouses of other children's pastors, and I hear the same story over and over. There's always more work than there is time to do it. I don't know that I've ever heard of a children's pastor who had loads of extra time on his or her hands." Rebecca leaned closer and put her hand on his again. "I just wonder if you're being idealistic. I have this feeling that you'll just end up at another great church overwhelmed with work there as well."

"I don't buy it, Rebecca. You're not at the office with me all day every day. You don't totally see all the stuff I've got to get done every week. You don't know all the meetings I have that completely suck the life out of me." Eric jumped up as if an idea just hit him. "Oh, and get this. Case and point, I was waiting for the right time to tell you this, but guess what Pastor hit me with on Tuesday? Saturday night services!"

If an entire body could frown, that's what Rebecca's body was doing at that moment.

"I know. I'm not thrilled with the idea either. Even if I took some time off on Thursday to make up for the extra hours, I'd still be gone all the time, and I'd never get all my work done." With a somewhat deranged look on his face, Eric shouted and shook his fist toward the ceiling, "If I can't get all my work done in four days at the office, what makes anyone think I could get even more done in three and a half?"

Rebecca crossed her arms and sank back into the couch, staring at the ceiling. After a brief silence, she looked across the coffee table at Eric who was pacing back and forth. "Eric, I'm not going to lie, I'm really not happy about Saturday-night services, especially with where we have been in this season of our lives. But I'm still not convinced. Putting your family first is a choice. It's supposed to be a priority. If we treat family as a priority, it affects everything else."

Eric looked a little agitated. "Rebecca, don't take this the wrong way." A voice in the back of Eric's head told him to proceed with caution. "What you say sounds really good in theory, but I really don't think you know what you're taking about."

Rebecca pointed her finger at him, "What's that supposed to mean? I may not be a children's pastor, but I still experience some of the things you do. It may not be networking meetings, budget planning, and curriculum development, but you try being a mom to three kids and manage all that that entails, keeping the house somewhat clean, keeping everyone fed, and trying to find some time for myself. I'm no stranger to priorities, Eric Newman."

Eric took a seat across from Rebecca. He wasn't sure if he was reading Rebecca correctly or not. Was she just being sassy, or was she really, really angry? "Honey, I don't mean to say that you don't understand what priorities are. I don't envy your job at all, and I'm so thankful for you; however, I feel that I'm in a position that if I make changes that intentionally put my family first, several things, several important and essential things, won't get done."

Rebecca cocked her head to the side and asked, "Things more important than EJ?"

"What?"

She enunciated each word quietly, "I'm asking if these very important things are more important than your son who loves his dad so much that he was positively crushed when you flaked out again on him."

"Rebecca, that's not fair."

Rebecca raised her voice, "Why not? Eric, he's your son, and you're missing it. Right now he wants you to be a part of his life, and in a few years, he might not. Honey, we could lose him if we don't seize these precious moments!"

Eric looked flustered. "I feel like I'm having an argument that doesn't make any logical sense to you. It's not black and white like that, Rebecca."

She looked him square in the eyes. "Just say it, Eric. Are the important tasks that you're afraid you won't be able to do more important than your oldest son?"

Eric felt painted into a corner. "No, of course not!"

Rebecca relaxed a little. "Good."

"What do you mean *good*?"

"Then if EJ really is more important than those work tasks, when faced with a choice between EJ and the task, you'll choose EJ," Rebecca said with smirk.

"Honey, it's just not that easy. You're making this too black and white. If I start dropping these tasks, I'll start letting people down. My performance will suffer noticeably. If it goes on too long, I'll be out of a job."

"Now you're being too black and white. I can't honestly believe that Pastor will up and fire you because a few tasks get dropped because you're making sure to not *neglect your family*. Maybe I'm being idealistic, but I think that if you make the choice to put us first, and you're willing to let things fall to the wayside for our sake, you will be surprised."

"What do you mean by that?"

"I'm just saying that living with your priorities in the right place may help you see some things you didn't see before. Maybe you'll see ways to get things done quicker, or maybe you'll see a totally different way to do them. Heck, maybe you'll see some things that you don't really even need to do anymore. I just have a feeling that God would honor that kind of decision. I don't think He'll stop the Sun in its place every day for you, but He'll help you be successful in spite of making sacrifices in your ministry."

"Well, that all sounds cute, but your 'feeling' doesn't sign my paycheck."

Rebecca made a face at Eric. "I'll pretend you didn't just say that. All I'm trying to say is that I'm not convinced we're done at New Hope. I think sending out resumes is a little premature."

"Maybe, but I think your pie-in-the-sky ideals are a little too theoretical for me. I'm not convinced that I can just make a split decision like you're suggesting, and then everything is going to be peachy keen. Something is broken, and it needs fixing."

Rebecca just shrugged her shoulders.

"So," Eric paused, searching his wife's eyes, "are we okay?"

"At this moment, we're okay, I think." With a smile, she pointed at Eric, "Consider yourself on probation." In a more serious tone she added, "I really like this interchange we had, but we didn't really decide anything."

Eric hung his head. "I know. I know. I've just got some more thinking to do. I need to figure this stuff out. I don't know what the answer is. I respect what you've said, but I'm not convinced that it's the answer for me, and I've got to know what that answer is."

"Sunday evening," Rebecca said.

"What?"

"After the kids are in bed."

"What are you talking about?"

"Sunday, after the kids are asleep, I want to know what we're going to do. I want to know what's going to change."

"*This* Sunday?" Eric whined.

"This Sunday. We can't live like this any longer. We have to put an end to it. We're not going to lose this family."

Eric swallowed hard. So much had happened to him in the past week, more than he had time to process. And as if that weren't enough, he had to decide what his next steps were going to be and make key decisions that would likely impact his family and ministry immediately.

He looked at Rebecca, and in a timid but resolute voice he said, "This Sunday."

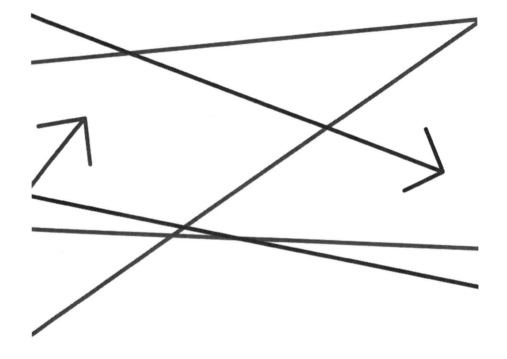

Chapter 5:
Order Your Priorities

MATT MCDANIELS

Have you ever felt overwhelmed by your ministry job? You're nodding your head, aren't you? Has the overwhelming nature of your work transferred into your home life? Has your family ever been affected by ministry-related stress? Am I painting a picture that is all too familiar to you?

Unfortunately, this is the nature of ministry that most called to serve the local church experience. Roles and responsibilities at church tend to bleed into other areas of our lives, and it's difficult to separate *work* from *time off*. Ministry often brings stress into our personal lives. Drawing boundaries between ministry and family is very difficult. Ministry jobs that once brought joy and excitement often leave us jaded and cynical. Why is this so?

We have all felt the excitement and joy of children's ministry. No matter what capacity we're involved, there are things that we see in those classrooms of children that we cannot see anywhere else. I can't name a more pure scene than watching a small child worshipping, not mimicking the motions going on around them or concerned with the eyes behind them, only concentrating on letting Jesus know that he or she really does love Him. I love watching those moments every weekend. I want to create that pure moment of worship in my classrooms every single week. That passion I have for helping children worship God pushes me harder each week. I spend a lot of time on our worship. I train our teams how to act and react during worship. I preview new songs and videos. I rotate music strategically to try to keep our worship fresh and growing. I regularly solicit feedback from volunteers and kids.

But this passion of mine takes up a lot of time. I could easily save a significant amount of time by simplifying our worship, and it would still be good. But my passion pushes me to strive beyond what is simply good.

Passion is a powerful force, one that we should have. Without passion, we're punching clocks until our time is up. Passion will cause excellence, and learning to transfer our passion into volunteers and children will cause excellence to multiply. We should love what we do, and we should make sure people know it. When people see us loving children's ministry, they will want to love children's ministry.

Donald Miller describes this in his book *Blue Like Jazz*. He describes how he hated jazz music until the moment he saw someone playing jazz on a saxophone. He saw someone in love with jazz. Eyes closed and lost in the music, the musician was experiencing something powerful. At that moment, Donald Miller wanted to love jazz music like that musician did, and since then, he has come to appreciate and enjoy jazz music. Similarly, this is what others need to see in us. Our display of passion shows everyone that we're taken with love for what we're doing, and this is contagious.

Passion is double sided though. The same passion that drives us toward excellence and love, can drive us into overworking and being totally stressed out. It can cause us to never turn down a project, over-schedule our time, and not pass projects to others who might not do things exactly like we would do them. Passion is good, but we must recognize the other side.

Whether we're in full-time ministry or serving as a volunteer, passion is usually what keeps us going. However, unless we say no to some things, cancel a few events, or delegate some responsibilities to others (even if you really love to do them), our passion is going to eat our lunch.

When I started working at my current church, I was naïve about passion. I was the third person hired at the church, and I had multiple responsibilities. I didn't call myself the children's pastor; I called myself *the slash man*. I was the children's pastor/television-show editor/computer technician/web developer/office assistant/janitor/anything-else-my-senior-pastor-needs-done man. I was young. I was excited. I had so much passion I could have bottled it and run a small country. I wasn't just passionate about children's ministry either; I had passion for it all. I loved producing the television show, building the website, and doing graphic design for the church. I was driven, and I let that drive take me wherever it wanted me to go. Unfortunately, that drive took me to a place that was awfully close to divorced and alone.

My wife and I had travelled 600 miles away from her closest friends and family members for this ministry job. I was putting in 60-70 hours a week leaving her absolutely alone except to eat and sleep. My passion and drive was leading me to place ministry as a higher priority than my wife.

I realized that I was simply following the same pattern from when I first got out of college. I was young and single and, honestly, I had little better to do than totally throw myself into ministry. It was fun, and I was passionate about what I was doing. Other than taking my future wife out on a date, I didn't have anything better to do. Looking back, I realize that even though I wasn't hurting anyone, my life was really unbalanced. Time may have been better spent investing in some friendships or even picking up a hobby. It certainly would have helped me set better boundaries for when I was to be married.

My priorities were out of alignment, and my wife and I headed down an unhealthy road. The confrontation was not very clear and straightforward. Instead of having a discussion about how I spent too much time at work or how I never paid full attention to her, we just started growing apart. My wife began to resent moving away from her friends and family, and I couldn't blame her. She did not understand that the cause of the separation was misplaced priorities, and neither did I. We were simply walking through the motions of life and slowly turning in different directions.

I had heard speakers talk about family being my greatest sermon. I'd heard messages about the most important kids in my ministry were my children at home, but my eyes chose not to see the reality of my situation. How could I be a *bad* husband or father if I was not doing anything bad? The problem is that I had determined my own definition of what a good husband was, and I was meeting the expectations of the definitions I had set. I wasn't committing adultery, I wasn't abusive, and we didn't appear to be dysfunctional. However, I never asked my wife what her definition of a good husband was.

I've come a long way from those days. A good friend and mentor helped me evaluate my priorities, and that exercise saved my life, or at the least, my marriage. Here's an example of my current priorities and how I live by them.

PRIORITY ONE: GOD

I am a Christ follower. I will develop an ever-growing relationship with Christ based on my love for Him. I will show Him my love through Bible reading, prayer, worship, and being a servant.

GOALS: I will read a minimum of one day from my *Bible in a Year* every day. This week I will find a person I do not know who needs help, and I will help him or her.

PRIORITY TWO: JENNY (MY WIFE)

I am a husband. I will develop an ever-growing relationship with Jenny based on my love for her. I will show her my love through quality time, gifts, acts of service, and words of affirmation.

GOALS: We will go out on a date night without kids at least once a month.

This week I will buy Jenny a surprise present and have it delivered to her.

PRIORITY THREE: ALARIC (MY SON)

I am a father. I will develop an ever-growing relationship with Alaric based on my love for him. I will show him my love through quality time, gifts, acts of service, and words of affirmation.

GOALS: I will pray for my son and lay him down for bed every single night.

This week I will take Alaric to the park and play whatever game he wants.

PRIORITY FOUR: WORK

I am the children's pastor at LifeBridge. I will serve the senior pastor at LifeBridge and develop his vision for the children's ministry. I will work hard to create a children's ministry that shows excellence, effectiveness, and relevance.

GOALS: I will do any responsibilities that are assigned to me by my pastor before I do anything else.

These are my priorities. I don't live these out every day, but having them written helps me to hit them more often than not. Sharing them with others helps keep me accountable. What about you? Have you ever verbalized your priorities and developed goals for them? What's stopping you?

If you've not done this, I'd highly encourage you to stop reading, pull out a pad of paper, and start jotting down what your priorities are. Don't write out your current reality; write out how you think things should be. Ask God to speak into your priorities. Bathe them in prayer. Measure them against God's Word. Invite your spouse to speak into what your priorities should be. Talk about them with your kids, some friends, and even your pastor. Ask them what a good employee, husband, father, and friend look like.

There is really no point in being the best husband that I could ever want, or the best dad that I could ever have, or the best employee that I could ever lead. I'm not my own husband; I'm Jenny's husband. I'm not my own dad; I'm Alaric's dad. See where this is going? Involve God in this conversation too. Find out the kind of follower He wants you to be as well. Write your goals down. Develop a definition for excellence, and order your priorities from most important to least. You will probably want to prioritize more than just your goals. Think of your typical week and the things you do. Put health, hobbies, friends, extended family, and ministry-outside-of-work on your list as well.

Below each of these priorities, put a group of three or four goals that are very measurable. Saying that I will show my wife that I love her through acts of service is not very measurable. Saying I will wash the dishes for my wife two times this week is very measurable. Create goals for the week or the month based on your priorities. Some goals, such as one night out a month with your spouse or praying with your children every evening before bed, produce significant returns. These are the kind of guardrails that will keep you in line relationally with the people that matter most. Discuss these with your spouse or people that hold you accountable, and set your goals together. Make them meaningful to everyone involved.

Some goals may not involve everyone. For instance, you might not tell your spouse every detail of every goal that involves him or her. Your commitment to take out the trash every day before your spouse has to ask may be something that serves her best without you communicating this goal ahead of time. However, that may be a goal that a friend is holding you accountable for. You may not share your goal to have a date night every week with your little son or daughter, but your spouse may help hold you accountable to that one.

Review your goals, and modify for the coming week. Every Monday I like to review my goals and set new goals for the week. With all of these goals, don't lose sight of the focus—hitting every goal you set for yourself isn't the end; it's a tool. Attempting to accomplish every goal is how you prioritize certain relationships and show love instead of neglect. My primary focus is to create an ever-growing relationship. That means, if my wife and I were closer last week than we are this week, I did something wrong. If I completed my goals but failed to get closer to my wife this week, then my goals are off, or I lost sight of what was most important. As you see which goals are effective and which ones are not, you will begin to see how you should spend your time.

Here are a few questions to get you started:
- What makes God the most proud of you?
- What makes your spouse most happy?
- What makes your child feel secure and loved?

Answering questions about those who are important to you can help you understand which things are most important to them.

When considering short-term goals, keep in mind your schedule for the following week. If you know you'll be spending more hours at the office or if you have a big event coming up, setting a goal to take the family to the lake on Saturday might be more appropriate than staying up after your wife goes to bed so you can do those dishes for her. If you're going to be busy during the weekend, take one of your children out to breakfast during the week.

Also, open up those lines of communication. If you have a week ahead with no free time, let your spouse know about your lack of time in advance so that he or she knows what is coming. Plan on doing something together before or after the week so he or she feels prioritized.

When you have plans and goals associated with your priorities, the only valid reason to not fulfill one would be because a higher-ranking priority gets extra attention. Higher priorities always trump lower-level priorities. That means, when push comes to shove and you have to make a choice between a priority five or a priority three, the choice has already been made. If you have standing plans with your friends and your manager calls in a favor, pull out your priority list. Which one is higher? If you have plans with your spouse and a friend calls you up with a great opportunity, remember your priority. Follow your priorities, and honor those most important to you. There is room for compromise or negotiation, but this should always be the exception and not the rule.

Our time on this planet is far too short. The common view is that most people spend their last days regretting how they spent their time in their earlier years. Maybe that's unavoidable, and on your final day, the only thing that matters is the time you spent with your spouse and kids. But I have to believe that we can make choices today that will give us the satisfaction of time well spent on that final day. Decide what is most important, and live your life in that frame of reference. Invite others to help you. Nothing is worth sacrificing our relationship with God. Nothing is worth losing our spouse or kids over, not money, not security, not even that "opportunity of a lifetime." The day we identify our priorities and begin to carry out our days in that context is the day we truly begin to live.

Your Eric Trap

Don't fall into the same trap as Eric. Go beyond reading inspirational words and stories, and measure your life and ministry against the traps many in ministry fall into as did Eric. Open up your journal or notebook, and take time to answer the questions below. Allow the principles in this chapter to translate into the context of your life and ministry.

If you are married, what is the temperature of your marriage? What is getting in the way of a healthy relationship with your spouse? What are two to three things you can do to improve your marriage?

If you have kids, what is the temperature of your relationship with them? What is getting in the way of a healthy relationship with your kids? What are two to three things you can do to improve these relationships?

Too often when we are with our families, we are not fully present. What steps can you take to be fully present with your family and make that time special?

We depend on the fuel gauge to tell us when we're almost out of gas. What gauge or indicator can you develop to alert you of when you're running low relationally with your family?

What are your kids learning about family and marriage by observing you as their parent?

Do you have a vision, mission, or goals for your family? Consider setting aside some time with your spouse to develop something like this in writing.

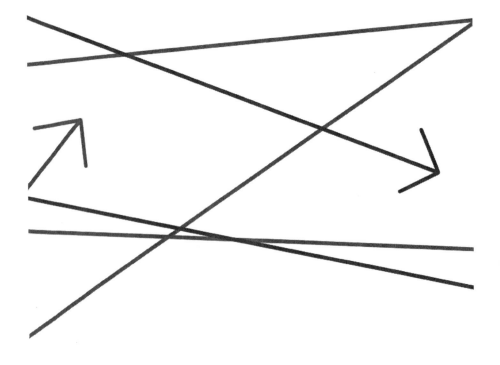

Conclusion: Happily Ever After?

Not Without Some Work.

JIM WIDEMAN

Eric is one hot mess! He's hardheaded, set in his ways, thinks everyone's out to get him, and he feels alone, confused, insecure, helpless, hopeless, and depressed. The truth is I know how he feels. I've walked in most, if not all, of the steps that he's walked out in the last few days. I have made every wrong choice Eric made. I hope that as you have read Eric's story, you could see yourself at times too. The trap that awaits Eric is the trap we all lay by our own choices. We win or lose by the way we choose.

Another trap to avoid is thinking that just because we make a right choice in the five areas mentioned here in this book, we don't have to continue to make those right choices in all five areas on a consistent basis. Eric has a lot of choices before him. I believe he's going to do the right thing and get those under control, but it's going to require three things from Eric.

First, it will require repentance. No change can be sustained without a change of behavior that comes from the heart. At the essence of repentance is the willingness and desire to do an about-face and travel in the opposite direction. Same actions always bring same results. When Eric chooses different actions, different thinking, different choices that come from true godly repentance, those will produce different outcomes for Eric and his family. But if Eric doesn't humble himself, he's headed for a fall.

Secondly, Eric has to choose to *do* the right thing. There is a big difference between wanting to do right and actually doing right. You have to do more than just talk about the right choices; you have to make the right choices. I can't count the number of times I've said, "I'm going to do this differently tomorrow," but tomorrow never comes. Our choices are important. They are important to God and our families, but mainly they are important to us.

The third thing Eric has to do is commit to continually making right choices. All of us have to determine to finish well. There is a lot of hype and fanfare given to starting things, and it is important that we get off to a good start in all we do. But how we finish is more important than how we start. My marriage and my ministry both started out rocky, but along the journey I realized it's more important to make right choices consistently in both of these areas, not just intermittently. Now my marriage and my ministry are what I am known for in the church world. Most of us think about habits negatively, but there can be good habits in our lives as well as bad ones. I choose to develop good ones.

As I watched the story of Eric unfold, I took his side on a few things until I saw what it was doing to his home and his ability to sustain longevity in the ministry. I know exactly how he feels because I've felt that same way a hundred times. I know some would question, "But, Jim, you've never thought about quitting the ministry, have you?"

Yes, I have. For a while I thought about it every Monday. There were some weekends I wanted to be off like everyone else. I wanted to go to a ballgame or even watch an entire game on TV in one sitting—thank God for DVRs! But I have seen firsthand the difference consistent good choices in every one of these five areas makes versus just making occasional good choices and throwing in the towel when times get tough.

When I first started in ministry, I worked for a wonderful pastor—G.D. "Jabby" Wilson. I'll never forget one of the things Brother Wilson told me. In twenty-five years of ministry, he had never seen anyone come in for marriage counseling without having at least one or all of these three areas of their lives messed up: their relationship with Christ, their finances, and/or their sex life. I can say that so far in my thirty-five years and counting, he has always been right.

In the same way, 100 percent of the leaders I mentor and coach have at least one of these five areas messed up: they are trying to do ministry alone; they haven't learned to delegate; they need to partner with families; they are measuring with the wrong ruler, and/or, most importantly, their priorities are messed up.

DON'T DO IT ALONE

God has sent us as leaders to prepare His people for works of service so the body of Christ may be built up. Every believer can do ministry. We need to see ourselves as overseers, not the only doers. I learned along my journey that there are people in my church who need to be needed more than I need the help. Once we locate those people, it's a blessing for both parties.

SERVE YOUR LEADER(S)

We must live and minister as ones under authority, not just with authority. When we love our pastors and leaders, we reflect the people we serve and the vision of the house. Jesus came to earth to represent his Father. I love what He said, "If you have seen Me, you have seen the One who sent Me." (John 14:9.) I want to represent my pastor well and reflect him in the children and student ministries I lead for him.

PARTNER WITH FAMILIES

Partnering with the family is not optional; it is mandatory. We are not just a bunch of yellows (the color that stands for the church, the light of the world) trying to get along and coexist with a bunch of reds (the color of the family, the heartbeat of God). We must become orange (two equal powers working together to produce something more powerful than either color on its own). In the early days of children's ministry, we told families, "You go to church, and we'll take care of your children." It didn't cross our mind to read our Bibles first and see that God's original plan for world evangelism and discipleship involved the family. We were wrong, so now we must partner with the family to help them train their children and teenagers for Christ. We need each other. The family needs the church, and the church needs the family. We must form a partnership and work together in a new way. Never forget that same action brings same results.

MEASURE WITH THE PROPER RULER

If we don't know how to measure true success and identify a win, we'll never know if we've truly achieved it. There are some sports I just don't enjoy. The reason I don't enjoy them is I don't know what the rules are. More specifically, I don't know how to keep score. I've found that once I learn how to keep score, I can learn the rules, the philosophies, and strategies of the game as I go and begin to enjoy it.

PRIORITIZE

Keep your priorities in order. Proverbs 28:2 says that when a country is rebellious, it's because it has many rulers; but a man of understanding and knowledge maintains order. I want to be that kind of leader, one of understanding and knowledge. To be that kind of leader, I have to maintain my priorities and keep them in the right order. No one can do this for me.

Eric has a lot of stuff out of Biblical order. He didn't get burned out from just working his days while he was off alone somewhere; he got overwhelmed. To be overwhelmed means one has lost the ability to break big tasks, assignments, or responsibilities into small, manageable bites. The Bible tells us that our steps, not our leaps and jumps, are ordered of the Lord. (Ps. 37:23.) The problem is we don't always think in steps.

When we look at Eric, we can clearly pinpoint where his priorities are messed up. Eric's relationship with Christ is in really bad shape, but that should be his first priority—to love the Lord his God with all his heart and all his soul and all his mind. (Mark 12:30.) For me, this is a fulltime job, not something I work on when I can. Also, Eric's family is in shambles. His marriage needs a lot of work; his kids need their Dad! Eric will have to work on these two priorities, or he'll become a casualty of the ministry. His ministry has a lot of things that need fixing (and hopefully we'll get around to that in future books), but right now he must choose first to survive in ministry while he makes his relationships with God and family right. After that, he will have to order the rest of his priorities himself. Priorities do change from time to time and throughout different stages and seasons of your leadership and ministry. For me, right now my third priority is my health. (I'll be writing more about that subject as well in future books, but I can say this much right now—we can't accomplish what God placed us on the earth for and finish well if we are dead. We have to take care of our bodies if we're going to finish well. Even if someone gets off to a bad start like I have, if that person is still alive, he or she still has an opportunity to make right choices in activity and eating on a consistent basis.)

I hope you'll take a little time after reading this book and do some evaluating of your own life (I sure did as I looked at Eric). The truth is there is a little bit of Eric in all of us, and when I'm completely honest with myself, I realize there is a whole lot more of Eric in me than I care to admit.

Here are a few questions to jumpstart you on the evaluation pathway:

Which of these five areas do you need to work on?

What's out of order?

Where are you doing ministry alone?

What are you doing that someone else can do?

What are you doing that's keeping you from doing what only you can, or should, be doing?

Where have you left out the family?

How can you include and build the family?

How do you measure success?

How do you define a win?

How do you celebrate success with your team?

Can you make a list of your priorities?

Is your list the same as God's priorities for you?

How are you doing with those priorities?

Are you a true reflection of the leaders you serve?

What traps have you set by your own bad choices?

These are important questions not just to ask now but on a regular basis!

We must remember that the ministry is all about developing people. We are not in the religion business; we are in the people business. I've never found a better way of building people than to enlist and involve them in the work of the ministry. A person serving others is the best way I've found to build disciples. Don't let your family suffer from not learning how to develop and delegate to others. It's not just about helping you and your family; it's about delegation, which leads to *duplication*, another word for *discipleship*.

Moses learned this the hard way. The reason his father-in-law, Jethro, showed up in the first place was because, like Eric, the choices Moses was making were adding a toll to his marriage and his family. Moses' wife took the kids and went home to daddy. But daddy brought her back and coached Moses on the art of delegation and duplication. It is a fascinating story to me.

I hope you've also learned from Eric that hard work isn't necessarily smart work. All of us need to work hard, but when I work as smart and as hard as I can, it always pays off. I hope Eric doesn't quit. He has a good pastor who loves him, and I believe he would help if Eric would swallow his pride and ask for help. The grass isn't always greener; it's just different grass. If Eric doesn't deal with his issues and choices, he'll just take his old challenges to the next ministry he works for.

God has placed Pastor Wheeler in Eric's life for a reason. I would not be the man of God, the husband, the dad, and the minister I am today without the five wonderful pastors God has placed in my life. Each of them deposited a big part of themselves in me, and I will be eternally grateful for that. God places us in another man's ministry to not only help and serve, but, in exchange, that pastor deposits a part of his giftings and helps shaping us for the long haul God has for us.

Eric has to burn the ships like the Vikings of old (i.e., quit talking and thinking about leaving every time there's a problem). I hope Eric also realizes a leader can't be down on his people if he is going to lead them effectively. A leader has to believe in his team. This is something a leader can't fake; his team knows when he's faking it. If a leader doesn't like the level his or her team is on, he or she must love them to their next level of leadership. I hope Eric will stop being weary in doing good things and choose joy. It is a choice. I can't control what happens in life, but I can control how I react and how I respond to what happens. I choose to do what the Word says. My attitude is under my control, and I have to master it.

More than just having a big vision, I hope that Eric learns how to cast that vision to others and let them help him. Vision is an amazing power. For example, one day I was pondering why I had never moved on to be a senior pastor instead I am still pastoring young people; but then I realized the answer. My vision won't let me quit. (Along the way, I realized I didn't have a big vision: a big vision had me!) If my vision won't let me quit, and if I can find ways to instill and grow that vision within others, then that vision will do the same for my team. It won't allow them to quit either. That's the power of a God-inspired vision.

Eric also needs to learn that he can't please everyone. There are some people in life that if I gave them a 100-dollar bill, they would complain because they wanted two fifties. Seek to please God, not man. I also hope Eric gets control of his fear; it's faith in reverse. Identifying where he's allowed fear to creep in will stop him from going backward and start him back in the right direction. I also hope Eric quits trusting his feelings; they are a bad guide and something he should never listen to.

There are a lot of people in Eric's life that God has placed there to help him. I hope he wakes up and sees that. I know that Bill would be glad to mentor and coach Eric, and he could learn a ton if he'd humble himself. Everyone does better with a coach. In the last five years that I've been coaching, I've found coaching is not only the most rewarding aspect of ministry I've ever done, but I've also found it is the most effective. I love conferences. I do. I'm a conference junkie. But most aspects of ministry can't be mastered in a few forty-five minute or one-hour sessions. Bill can also help Eric see that everything is not someone else's fault. Eric has brought all of this on himself. Yes, the devil is having a field day with this young man, but Eric needs to man up.

Eric has a lot of major decisions ahead, and if he doesn't start making some deposits, his ministry is going to begin floating bad checks. Ministry is just like a bank account: it has to make spiritual deposits first. Faith deposits first and then writes the checks. We minister out of our overflow. Eric, God love him, is ministering out of debt. Without repentance, he's headed for spiritual bankruptcy. I've found that I can't trust myself to make major decisions when I'm as tired as Eric is. This is the time for him to learn to be like King David and encourage himself in the Lord. Leaders have to get creative in learning how to keep themselves built up, encouraged, and growing in their faith. I've always heard what's good for the goose is good for the gander. Plus, every leader needs to be willing to be an example.

If I knew Eric's address, I'd send him a copy of *Beat The Clock,* my little book on time management. There are so many wonderful tools that we have around to help us manage ourselves. If I had had a smart phone when I was his age . . . oh, wait a minute, I did! And I used it to remind me of what I needed to do. The important thing about a smart phone is to remember to not do dumb things with it. A leader's tools should help him do more, not cause him to do less! Never let your tools become toys.

Not only has God placed a wonderful friend and mentor, and a wonderful pastor in Eric's life, but also God has blessed Eric with a wonderful wife. I hope Rebecca hangs in there. Plus, Eric is so out of touch with EJ. I hope EJ has surrounded himself with the right friends. When kids can't depend on us, they look for others they can depend on, especially when they're EJ's age. Eric and Rebecca need Pastor Wheeler's help. They could also benefit from Florence and her husband as marriage mentors. Isn't it amazing how self absorbed we can become when we don't see help like Florence standing in front of us? It's so obvious she cares a lot for Eric and could take over his schedule if he'd let her. It blows me away how many insecure people I know in the ministry. Eric and Rebecca have a lot of work ahead. It isn't going to be easy, but if they'll both seek God and stick to their vows, they can turn their family around and make it their greatest sermon.

The church has become Eric's mistress, and he must allow Pastor Wheeler to help him get his priorities in the right order. Eric can't keep his priorities if he can't identify what they are. That's the starting place.

I hope Eric will remember Bill's advice and measure his ministry the right way. We can't measure our success by the size of our ministry, our gadgets, or our check-in systems but by life change. Bill's four points are huge. Here they are again:

- Always support your pastor. If you find yourself in a place when you no longer do, it's time to find another pastor whom you can support.
- The tools we use do not measure our effectiveness, but life change that results from the tools we use will measure it accurately.
- Life change is not measured in weeks and months but rather in years and decades.
- Your family is the best indication of your success in life and ministry.

Finally, I hope Eric gets a copy of this book. I hope Eric gets these things right. I hope you do too.

May I pray for you?

Heavenly Father, I thank You for those who read this book. May Your Holy Spirit guide them to make the changes You are speaking to them now. Thank You for equipping those You call and helping them finish strong and get these five things right so they can be the leaders You want them to be. In Jesus' name, amen.

About the Authors

Jim Wideman

@jimwideman
Teacher of Kids and Teens and those
who teach them. I'm in love with
one woman and many guitars!

Jim Wideman Fan Page

twitter.com/jimwideman

brojim@jimwideman.com

www.jimwideman.com

 Out on a date with mrs@jimwideman. The best decision I ever made other than accepting Jesus was marrying her many moons ago

 Huge thanks to @nlcast- James Kennison for doing the cover artwork for "The Eric Trap" it looks great! Also special thanks to Beth DeLemos Consulting for additional art direction and book layout!

 Heading over to my favorite singer @yancynotnancy & my favorite banner guru- @mommentummedia's house to see my handsome little grandson. He's a dude!

 My youngest daughter @wmakeup & @dustinprude are married. Could not be more proud of them than I am right now.

 Last but not least thanks to all the many infuse folks-you have made me a better leader I am so glad that you are in my life!

Sam Luce

@samluce Utica, NY
Christ Follower, Husband,
Father, Campus Pastor,
Family Pastor, #kidmin

 facebook.com/samluce

 twitter.com/samluce

 samluce.com

samuelluce@gmail.com

Sam Luce
Happiest Day of my life was getting married to
@sandrasluce She is more beautiful than words.

Sam Luce
Just celebrated my 14th year as kidspastor of
Redeemer.tv What an honor!

Mike Servello
@samluce your kids are getting so big can't believe They
are 7, 5 and 2 already time flies.

Sam Luce
Get to speak at a bunch of conferences this fall. So
humbling to be able to share what God has done!

Kenny Conley

@kennyconley
Husband to Sara. Father to Titus and
Genevieve. NextGen Pastor to
Gateway (Austin, TX)

 facebook.com/kennyconley

 twitter.com/kennyconley

 childrensministryonline.com

Kenny@childresministryonline.com

 @kennyconley You're having a girl? Congrats! They are such a blessing... and expensive!

 RT @jimwideman @kennyconley You're having a girl? Congrats, they're a blessing / Thank you! Sara and I are so excited. First Conley girl in over 64 years!

 @saraconley Happy anniversary baby! These have been the best 12 years of my life! Looking forward to the next 12!

 Hey #kidmin! I just changed the look and layout of my blog. Click over to childrensministryonline.com and check it out! You know you want to!

Kristin Englund

@englundk
Family Ministries Director, Elementry
Education Grad, KidLead trainer, beach
loving coffee drinker, Leadership junkie

 facebook.com/englundk

 twitter.com/englundk

englundk@gmail.com

 Man do I love my job as Family Ministries Director at Fair Haven. If you live in southwest MI, you should visit us or one of our sites around thearea! www.fhmin.org

 Just saw the "Bodies Revealed" exhibit at the museum in GR. Gross, yet interesting. Reminds me of my years studying Science Education @GVSU.

 @englundk Real proud of your church going multi-site not easy for 50-year-old church. Love your commitment "New churches reach new people."

 There are challenges and joys being someone in church leadership in their 20's. It's "fun"when coworkers remind me I could be their child. 1 Timothy 4:12 has never rung more true!

Sherri Epperson

@sherriepperson
Follower of Jesus, volunteer leader in
Family Ministry (my passion), an
administrator in architectural
antique design.

 facebook.com/sherriepperson

 twitter.com/sherriepperson

 SLHSLE@aol.com

 Spent the weekend with @sherriepperson's kids Pastor. Great guy. Great church check them out on the web http://www.calvarycc.org/

 Having a proud mama momment. Just got back from a gymnastics meet. My twin girls did great. So proud of them!

 Watching "The Sound of Music" with my husband. How lucky am I?

 Working at my antiques shop going over my script for Sunday. Love serving my church.

Craig Gyergyo

@craiggyergyo
Husband, father, kids' ministry director,
& karaoke singer.

 facebook.com/craig.gyergyo

 twitter.com/craiggyergyo

 **gyergyoc@yahoo.com**

 ..If I were to sing you a song right now it would be "Love Rescue Me" from U2's Rattle and Hum. (Could I match the passion of the original? Of course. The falsetto could be problematic, however - albeit entertaining.)

 "If there is leftover pizza or cake in the house, then there is a 99.9% chance that I will eat something that comes in the form of a slice for breakfast."

 RT @craiggyergyo The two years I spent in Infuse with @jimwideman helped me grow more as a leader than anything I've experianced.

 Leaving my job as a teacher and going on staff at New Hope Church http://hopepres.com/ was one of the best decisions I ever made!

Deana Hayes

@DeanaH
Daughter of the King, wife, mother,
grandmother and children's pastor.

 facebook.com/deana.hayes1

 twitter.com/deanah

 deana4kids@sbcglobal.net

 RT @DeanaH: Great conversation with @jimwideman at #kidmin11

 Just hit the ten year mark at my church http://www.avonlightandlife.org/ so amazing to see my kids grow. Love my church!

 I think being a grandmother has to be the greatest thing ever!

 Staff Christmas dinner all wrapped up! Now I can take down the Christmas trees.

Matt McDaniels

@cpMattMcD
Christian, Husband,
Father, Children's Pastor... in order.

 facebook.com/cpmattmcd

 twitter.com/cpMattMcD

 matt.mcdaniels85@gmail.com

 Can't believe I get to serve as the kids pastor at my church! Love Lifebridge. Check them out on the web http://www.lifebridge.tv/

 RT @jennymcdaniels How about a date night Friday? //Proud of you for putting your priorities in order

---

 Just picked up some sweet new corals for my saltwater aquarium! I love my "old man hobby!"

 Hanging out with Alaric! I'm not bias when I say that he is the coolest kid on the planet.

The End

...or is it?

Check out TheEricTrap.com/MoreEric for bonus Eric Trap content.

Looking for more information about
Jim Wideman`s Infuse Coaching program?

Log on to **www.jimwideman.com** and click on the infuse tab!

Still have questions email us @ **theClub@jimwideman.com**

Each of the Authors of this book have been impacted by
infuse; you can too!

Every one of us has a little Eric Newman in us at
some point or another. Perhaps this book identified
the trap you've unknowingly fallen into. Join the Eric
Trap community online for additional book content,
resources and a place to tell your story.

Visit TheEricTrap.com/MoreEric

CPSIA information can be obtained at www.ICGtesting.com
Printed in the USA
LVOW10 155 9240612

287425LV00016B/263/P